Fashion

From haute couture to streetwear; key collections, major figures and crucial moments that changed the course of fashion history from 1890 to the 1990s

contents

1

the house of worth – fathers of couture

1

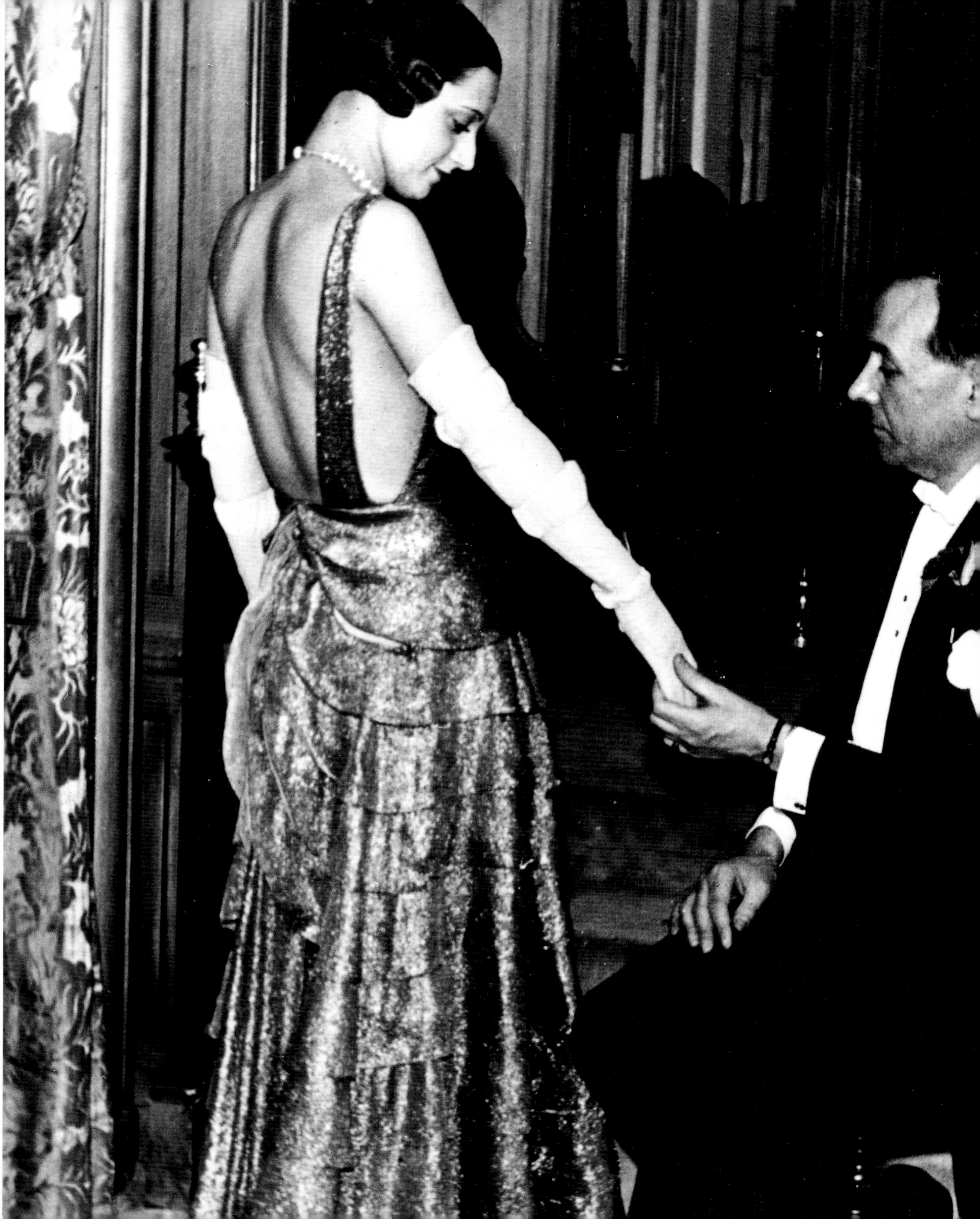

French haute couture was started by an Englishman named Charles Frederick Worth in the 1850s. He came from a family of Lincolnshire solicitors who had no connection with the clothing industry whatsoever.

Worth was born in the small market town of Bourne in Lincolnshire on 13 October 1825. He was just 11 when his father's drinking and gambling ruined the family business, and his father and mother separated. This spelt the end of the boy's education and he became an apprentice in a printworks. The work was dull and dirty. Worth hated it, but stuck it out for a year.

Eager to better himself, Worth raised the fare to London by making and selling Easter bonnets. Once there, he served an apprenticeship at the Swan & Edgar department store, for the next seven years living and working at the company's Piccadilly Circus premises, sleeping under the counter.

In 1845, Worth moved to the exclusive Regent Street silk dealers Lewis & Allenby, who had just been appointed mercers to Queen Victoria. Constantly striving to improve himself, he read widely and spent a great deal of his free time in the National Gallery, which had recently moved to Trafalgar Square. There he studied the fabrics and costumes depicted in art.

However, Worth's job was selling textiles, not making clothes. He became increasingly frustrated, and at the age of 20, he took the risk of quitting his job at Lewis & Allenby and headed for Paris. He had just £5 in his pocket, which his mother had borrowed from relatives, and he could not speak a word of French.

His first two years in Paris were fraught with difficulties. It was more than a year before he had learnt enough French to do shop work again. For a year, he worked in a dry goods store. Then he presented himself at No. 83 rue Richelieu, at Gagelin, Paris's most prestigious silk mercer who did regular trade with Lewis & Allenby in London. They gave him a job and suddenly he found himself at the centre of Paris's fashion world. He stayed and worked there for the next 11 years.

But Worth was as far as ever from the world of dressmaking which, in France as in England, was an exclusively female profession. He dealt only in fabric, the male side of the business. The political situation in France was also unstable. In his first four years at Gagelin, Worth saw the Bourbon monarchy fall, the establishment of the Second Republic, the rise of Napoleon III and the proclamation of the Second Empire.

Under Napoleon III, Paris was rebuilt and became the centre of world attention. Louis-Napoleon was keen to secure the friendship of Great Britain. The two countries became allies in the Crimean War in 1853. State visits were exchanged in 1855 and everything English became fashionable. Even Napoleon III's mistress, Elizabeth Howard, was English.

Gagelin supplied fabrics for the trousseau of Napoleon's bride, the Empress Eugénie. This gave Worth his introduction to the new court. Eugénie, a commoner by birth, set the tone for the Second Empire. A lowly birth, like Worth's, did not prevent you from getting on. The court favoured up-and-coming bankers and industrialists, rather than the old aristocracy. But, above all, it favoured beautiful women.

At Gagelin, Worth became acquainted with the most fashionable women of the day. He arranged the fashion shows, where young models showed off the latest fabrics which had been made up into shawls. He began making dresses for one of the models, Marie Augustine Vernet. Compared with the fussy fashions of the day, Worth's dresses were simple creations, designed primarily to show off the fabric of the shawl worn over them. Soon Gagelin's fashionable customers were demanding that he make dresses for them too. Gagelin were horrified. Dressmaking was

previous page The House of Worth flourished through generations; his grandson Jean Charles Worth was chief designer from 1910 to 1935

left Charles Worth with a model in one of his evening dresses, 1889

right An illustration by Paul Meras entitled *The Meeting in the Park* from the magazine *La Gazette du Bon Ton* (1914) featuring an evening dress designed by Worth

right *La Coquette Surprise*, an illustration by A.E. Marty of an evening dress by Worth, from the pages of *Gazette du Bon Ton* 1912

considered beneath them. But their customers were among the most influential women in France and they had no choice but to let Worth set up a small dressmaking department.

No other dressmaker in Paris could compete with Worth. Through Gagelin, he had access to the finest fabrics. He even knew the manufacturers, so he could order special fabrics and the patterns he wanted to be made up. As he had no formal training in tailoring, he was not inhibited with old ways of doing things. And he was obsessed with getting the garments to fit the wearer perfectly, to show the woman's body off to its greatest advantage.

In 1851, Worth married his model and inspiration, Marie Vernet, and Gagelin exhibited some of his silk dresses at the Great Exhibition. They won a gold medal; Worth's genius was now recognised in his homeland. France's answer to the Great Exhibition was the Exposition Universelle of 1855. There, again, Worth won first prize.

These two exhibitions brought numerous foreign clients – particularly Americans – to Gagelin. They found it very convenient to be able to have the finest fabrics made up into clothes on the spot. Worth also sold patterns and model gowns to foreign stores, so that they could produce identical garments when they returned home.

Although Gagelin was making huge profits from the business Worth was generating, Worth remained a mere *premier commis* – or first salesman. Promotion was denied him. So he quit and went into business with another *premier commis,* a Swede named Otto Bobergh. In 1858, Worth & Bobergh opened from Worth's first floor apartment at No. 7 rue de la Paix with a staff of 20 seamstresses.

Many of Worth's clients followed him from Gagelin. His creations were seen and applauded at court. But having a male couturier was still seen as

left A 1920 outfit by Worth from the pages of *Gazette du Bon Ton*

right The Empress Eugenie in a dress by Worth at the Universal Exhibition in Paris in 1867, on the arm of the Tzar of Russia

something shocking, so Worth was denied royal patronage. To overcome this, Worth sent his wife to visit Princess Pauline von Metternich, the wife of the Austrian ambassador and a favourite at court who was known for her daring pranks. Marie showed the princess some of Worth's sketches and she immediately ordered a morning dress and an evening gown.

Worth charged less than 300 francs each for the dresses, but he decided to take a gamble. He made the evening gown out of a white tulle spangled in silver. It was garnished with daisies and pink hearts in bunches of wild grass, veiled with more tulle.

The silver-spangled tulle was completely new and cost more than 300 francs alone. But this gamble paid off. Princess Pauline was so delighted with the gown that she wore it to the state ball at the Tuileries. It even caught the eye of the Empress Eugénie and, the next morning, Worth was summoned to the palace.

This caused consternation. Worth did not have the knee breeches and silk stockings that etiquette demanded. The best he could muster was the regular businessman's frock coat. It would have to do.

Worth won the order and he made a deal with the silk mills in Lyon. They would supply him with the finest silks for the Empress, provided he pushed brocade which had undergone something of a slump recently.

Unfortunately, the Empress did not like brocade and refused to wear Worth's creations. But Worth persuaded the Emperor that it would be diplomatic if the royal couple curried favour with staunchly republican Lyons. Napoleon III ordered his wife to wear Worth's gowns, which began a new fashion for brocade. This gave Worth tremendous influence with the silk mills of Lyon and other fabric manufacturers who vied for his patronage. It also gave him control over the Empress and the power to set the fashion for the whole of the court.

In 1860, Worth & Bobergh became renowned as the dressmakers to the Empress Eugénie, the most fashionable woman in Europe. The other Parisian houses tried to dent their reputation by spreading rumours that Worth & Bobergh, the only male-run dressmakers, was a brothel where the most indecent things went on. But this did not damage them at all. Every detail of the Empress' gowns was reported in the newspapers around the world. Soon orders were coming in from as far away as New York.

The Empress renewed her wardrobe twice a year. She gave her old gowns to her ladies in waiting, who sold them on to America and elsewhere. Because of the exceptionally high quality of his work, Worth soon had a monopoly on what the Empress wore. So, effectively, he dominated fashion world-wide.

The rue de la Paix became the centre of the fashion industry. Any women who expected to attend one of the Empress' balls would shop there. Each season during the Second Empire there were 130 balls, and it is estimated that over £1,000,000 was spent on ball gowns each year. Worth went through thousands of metres of silk and tulle to dress his clientele for each ball. He struggled to make every dress different, but his early study of costume in art was a constant source of inspiration.

Worth could really let his imagination run riot for the fancy-dress balls and masquerades which were becoming popular. He costumed his customers as characters from mythology, history and paintings, and he

also made some glamorous renditions of national costumes. The Duchess de Morny was attired by Worth as the Morning Star in silver-spangled tulle with a diamond star on her head.

However, Worth's most famous creation was the peacock dress he made for the Princess de Sagan to wear at the Bal des Bêtes in 1864. The head-dress looked like a small peacock and the train was covered in peacock feathers. Worth's son Jean-Philippe designed a similar peacock dress in 1903 for Lady Curzon, wife of the Viceroy of India.

Until Worth, dressmakers had been paid a pittance and often took a loss on a gown to hold on to an influential client. Once he was established, Worth deliberately set out to make his clothes 'the most expensive in the world'. The simplest gown cost 1,600 francs – £60, a great deal in those days. The most expensive was 120,000 francs – £5,000. But to wear a Worth proclaimed that you were wealthy and the nouveau riche, who were in the ascendancy during the Second Empire, clamoured for them.

Worth was responsible for several innovations. He dropped the waistline to hips and made a dress where the skirt and bodice were in one piece, without a waistline seam joining them. He raised hemlines, which

had brushed the ground since 1830. The Empress Eugénie like to take long walks in the countryside and was annoyed by the amount of mud her skirts picked up. So in 1863, Worth sheared ten centimetres off her skirts, raising the hem clear of the ground but leaving the Empress' ankles demurely covered. He also abandoned the bonnet that had been in fashion since the 1790s and got his own in-house milliner to make broad-brimmed hats that showed off the wearer's hair.

These new fashions were launched by Worth's models at the racecourse at Longchamps, making the race meeting less of a sporting event and more of a fashion show. He caused a sensation when he sent his wife and the Princess von Metternich there 'undressed'. They went without the shawls or cloaks which, until then, women had worn outdoors. Worth felt these hid his creations. But two weeks after, Marie and the Princess turned up *déshabillé,* shawls and cloaks had been abandoned by the fashionable women who inhabited the grandstand.

Worth then staged another coup by abandoning the crinoline and introducing the puff skirt, and exaggerating the *derriere* with a bustle. Many found this shocking, but Worth was such a force in the world of fashion that he held sway.

Although he refused to have his sketches published in magazines, his work was copied all over Europe and America. Despite this unlicensed competition, by 1870 Worth was employing 1,200 seamstresses, turning out hundreds of dresses a week and making a profit of over £40,000 a year.

Every client, except the Empress, was required to come to the salon for measurement and fitting. The rue de la Paix was crammed with carriages. No one – not even the most notorious courtesan – was turned away, provided they were able to pay. The women would have to parade up and down in front of Worth while he watched the way they walked. They were not allowed to express their own opinion. Worth would decide what suited them and decide what they were going to wear without even a consultation. His reputation was such that even the most noble ladies in the land submitted to his authority.

Then disaster struck. The 1870 Franco-Prussian War ended in defeat for Napoleon III. The Second Empire was over. The royal insignia was ripped from No. 7 rue de la Paix by a mob. The Empress Eugénie escaped to England with some of her gowns. With their most influential client gone, Worth & Bobergh closed. Bobergh decided the game was up and dissolved the partnership. With his share of the money, he returned to Sweden, bought a castle and married an actress. But Worth hung on.

Paris was besieged by the Prussians and Worth turned his salon into a hospital. He reopened for business in March 1871, but closed during the Commune and fled with his family to Le Havre. They returned in June to find the Tuileries burnt down and Worth's second most valuable client, the Princess von Metternich, packing to return to Austria.

left Beach resort wear from 1931 including two outfits by Worth, the white linen dress on the left and floral print creation second right

Requête de Worth...

left From French *Vogue* in June 1947, an advertisement for a perfume from the House of Worth

Even if he were to return to England, Worth would have required French fabrics and the haberdashing skills he had found in Paris. He had little choice but to stay. However, with the court now gone, Worth soon found himself in an even more powerful position. Orders flooded in from around the globe. It was Worth's fashions the world was interested in, not the celebrities who wore his creations.

American financier J.Pierpoint Morgan bailed out the ailing French economy and, in 1877, took his second wife Frances to visit Worth. Like other Americans, she was delighted to find a Parisian couturier who could speak English. From then on, each season, Worth would send her clothes to New York by steamer. Morgan never queried the size of the bill.

Worth also conducted a lively business with the remaining crowned heads of Europe, and even introduced the Princess line in honour of Britain's Princess Alexandra.

Worth had developed all the trappings of the modern couture house – the presentation of spring and autumn collections, live models, the creation of exclusive designs and the selling of toiles and paper patterns to foreign firms who could make their own garments abroad to his design. Actresses particularly flocked to his salon.

Worth's two sons, Jean-Philippe and Gaston, followed him into the business. While they supervised the salon, Worth himself, now wealthy again, spent his time building a chateau at Suresne. In 1885, he visited England for the first time in 40 years. First, he went to the Isle of Wight, which Queen Victoria and Alfred Lord Tennyson had made fashionable, then travelled to Farnborough to visit the exiled Empress Eugénie. Although he supported his parents financially for the rest of their lives, he did not visit Bourne, his birthplace.

Although Worth had lived most of his life in France, he retained his British passport to the end. Despite his wife's lifelong attempt to convert him, he never became a Catholic. And he turned down all honours, even the Légion d'Honneur, claiming that achievement was its own reward.

On 10 March 1895, Charles Worth died of pneumonia in Paris. He was 69. His sons continued to run the house until 1910, when Gaston's son Jean Charles took over as chief designer. Roger Worth took over when Jean Charles retired in 1935. Roger himself retired in 1952.

Two years later, Maurice Worth accepted a take-over bid from rival couture house Paquin, ending the independence of Paris's oldest and most enduring fashion house.

left A 1938 evening coat by Worth in moire (a watered silk fabric) and manufactured by Rémond

the 2 birth of the bra

The invention of the bra came at a turning point in history for women both in their dress and their destiny, and its development is inextricably linked with events in the 20th Century. The bra tells the story of the ongoing quest for comfort, freedom of movement and style in women's fashion. The optimum shape of the breast for each era is a manifestation of what was happening in the story of women's emancipation; women's requirements for comfortable, practical brassieres have been influenced by their own needs and desires. The size gap between bra and pants is an accurate barometer of liberalism of the times, but factors such as availability of new materials, developed during the wars and the space programme, have influenced design and activity.

There is a pattern in the 20th Century, influenced by the birth of the bra, of the denial of the female form, followed by times of pretence and padding, a most reliable indicator of the swing back to the kitchen or whenever there has been a backlash to feminism. Women's relationship to their underwear has always been erotic. The appearance and shape of the breast is greatly influenced by social and even philosophical issues, in film and advertising as well as in 'reality'. Where that begins and ends in the world of bras is largely between a girl and her conscience.

Until after the First World War, women's breasts were pushed up from underneath by laced bodices, (there were no cups) so that all their wares were on show. Children came out of swaddling clothes and into a busk, the 'shell' necessary to create the hourglass shape. Whatever the age of the wearer, the mature silhouette was favoured, so copious amounts of padding were placed in the many layers of underclothes worn by women. At the start of the 1890s, the most extreme form of corsetry was in evidence. Women of the late Victorian era were required to be covered from throat to toe, so the silhouette was most suggestive. A women's breasts had previously been the focal point of their costume, but now cleavage was taboo, so frills, inflatable balloons or even horsehair were used, to make up for what the eye could not directly see.

The subtext to modest was 'voluptuous' and this bulk, in incapacitating women, thus rendered them simply decorative. Uselessness was a positive attribute which set an *haute bourgeoise* apart from other women. Treated as a toy, being reserved for erotic play and procreation was the highest accolade. If they adhered to what was the fashion of the day, it is astonishing that women ever did more than this, but many chose to and many had to.

previous page Jane Russell in *The Outlaw*, with the bra designed by the film's producer Howard Hughes based on a cantilever principle he had developed in aircraft design!

left The early 20th Century hour glass figure, achieved with laced bodices, whalebones and padding

The hourglass figure was achieved by whalebones not only at the waist, but vertically pushing the chest forwards, the posterior back and tiny bones ensured that the chin was thrust forward, all adding up to the grotesque 'S'shape. The big heavy skirts they wore added to their isolation by keeping others outside their personal space, but, when crusading health experts sought to convince women of the dangers of this fashion, and the toll on their bodies of being laced in and trussed up, women dismissed them as either freaks or exponents of peculiar avant-garde morals. So much for the male conspiracy; the risks of wearing corsets ranged from infertility, damage to internal organs, deformities of the self and the offspring, not to mention the unsavoury connotations of dressing young women up to look 40 or 50 and the social conspiracy of pretending that women that age could not be trusted alone with a man, who may not be able to help turning animal at the sight of curves.

Despite the obvious discomfort and physical disadvantage of such costume, women still managed to achieve amazing feats – mountaineering and exploring desert terrain, playing sports and swimming, though probably less energetically on the whole than competitors today. After the First World War, women had proved their worth in doing the jobs left vacant by the men called up and killed in the war and because with women's suffrage and increasing interest in sports such as cycling and tennis there was a real demand for practical clothes. The evolution of the bra is a visual testimony of the quest for freedom, the unprecedented value placed on a thin bodyshape and ultimate demand for quality from the days when these concerns were the prerogative of the elite to the day when it is a concern for all.

There was also for a while, a period of dressing down after the apocalypse of World War I. Fashion started on its journey to androgyny and youthful ideal and there was another entirely new phenomenon which was to propel this notion – Hollywood. Actresses like Theda Bara were wearing scandalous creations and the illusion was that underwear was unnecessary and unattractive. Designers like Paul Poiret were playing with a completely new set of values – the Empire line, the hitherto intellectual notion of eastern inspired trousers and the sweater. Lucile had toyed with similar creations in London before the war for a very select few, and both designers hit upon the idea of lingerie in beautiful luscious fabrics and colours. Corsets now flattened, covering the same area, like a prototype corselette, with lots of primitive elastic and rubber.

The bra made its first appearance, supposedly, when a young girl called Mary Phelps Jacobs made one strictly pro-tem for a dance out of hankies and pins. She lost out though because being 14 and sweetly naive, she sold the patent to Warners for just $1500.

Early bras were not sized efficiently, but they struck a chord with the hunger for things modern and the emancipated young woman. In the 20s, everything was pared down to the bare minimum, legs were on show, diaphanous fabrics were used and really energetic pastimes were utterly 'it'. Flattening corsets developed into more discreet items, helped by better elastic and brode fabrics, mainly in pink. Wildly coloured tiny bra and French knicker sets in Rayon had just the right amount of hard hit for the

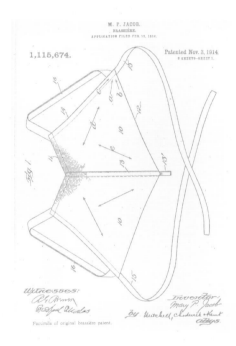

left The patent for the first bra filed on 12th February 1914 by Mary P. Jacobs, and registered 3rd November

below A chorus girl from the Ziegfeld Follies of 1920 showing the 'flattening' effect of the early bra

smokin' drivin' votin' young things showing off the tops of their stockings to the beat of the Black Bottom and the Charleston. Many were influenced by Josephine Baker, who had been known to keep her bosom up with a sash or even to make a mere gesture of covering her breasts with a garland of papier-mache bananas. Flappers' memoirs are full of tales of home-made solutions to the problem of feminine curves in a decade of boyish ideals. Tight bandaging was popular.

In the 30s the stars of Hollywood dictated the bodyshape. The bosom was interestingly emphasised by careful fitting over the front and the appearance of the bare back. The strict Hays code forbade any explicit show of cleavage, so Glamour was defined by tight fitting satin and silk evening clothes and the kind of eroticism camouflaged by jaunty dance routines and Ziegfeld's name. In European films, stars like Anny Ondra were routinely pictured by the likes of Hitchcock in their scantiest, in order to heighten the moment of tension and to add an extra dimension of vulnerability to the heroine.

Publ. M. NOIRCLERC

Ch. Lemmel

Scandale

GAINES
CEINTURES
SOUTIEN-GORGE

left The 50s Hollywood glamour queen Jayne Mansfield personified the bra-driven emphasis on the bust

far left From the French magazine *Femina* in 1946 – illustrations for underwear became an art form

During the war, when things were hard and luxuries were hard to come by, British and American governments backtracked on initial decisions and allowed women bras and lipsticks to raise morale. Women had sleeker figures due to the wartime diet, but the underwear that women got into in better times was complicated, somehow signalling (as female dressing had done before emancipation) that women could pamper themselves, the days of hard slog were over. Wishful thinking maybe, that women would disappear from the work market now they weren't needed, or confine their labour to girl's jobs. Unadulterated glamour and femininity were the bywords, and the strapless evening gown and the truly over the top swimsuit were the order of the day. As in the 80s the big shouldered suit with very defined bust gave way to evening fantasy. The strapless bra was essential to the mystique and came along just in time for the creation of the New Look, which took much of its influence from the fashions of Worth and the mid-19th Century.

The silhouette of the 40s was structured, bony and hard. The 'living bra' of the 50s was all womanly flesh by contrast. Bras had never been so elaborate or promised so much. The sweater girls had had their own 'whirlpool' stitched bras and in the 50s with Jayne Mansfield and Anita Ekberg in mind, the cantileverage and weapon-like silhouette make it apparent that the designers of aircraft and bras were men living out very Freudian and aggressive fantasies, with universal appeal. Despite the shape and tension of the bras, a very popular selling point was that it was so comfortable you forgot you were wearing it and they were so beautiful, it was a shame to hide them. Models were frequently pictured in the street in their underwear – this may account for the 80s trend of using the bra for outer wear.

It was at this time that the manufacturers invented cup sizes, Warners being the first. Now the increasingly educated and discerning female buyer could demand a better fit for her money. Women were now established wage earners in their own right, and it showed in their pursuit of subtle, elegant clothes with a more assured, simple shape.

Sportswear really took off in this period and its influence shows in the wearing of trousers, playsuits and swimwear, which all relied on a clever emphasis of the bust for the look of relaxed femininity of the day. Against the grain of the Depression and dearth of work, the trick was to look playful and happy. The breast was therefore pert and perky, and bras and pants were by now seen as the norm.

Candeur de *Jeunesse*

BRETELLES ÉLASTIQUES

la plus belle poitrine ... la plus naturelle

above A 1960 'prettiest is most natural' bra, moving away from the strictures of the agressive 1950s

The 60s just like the 20s brought the young androgynous figure back. To be youthful was the ultimate and woe betide those who were too old or too prim to discard all the trappings of 50s – the structured bra, the girdle and stockings and suspenders. The ever-increasing choices in man-made fibres revolutionised underwear as easy care rayon had in the 20s. The emergence of the first commercially produced Lycra products popularised the bodystocking and brightly coloured nylon sets of underwear were cheap and plentiful. Bare legs, bare chests and tiny pants signified the biggest gaps in underwear history. Liberalism and childlike ignorance of the difference between the sexes brought a temporary trend for unisex underwear.

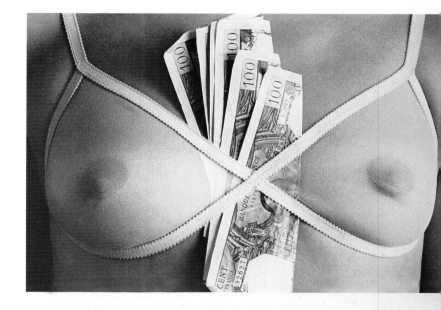

Imaginez-vous plus agréable manière de gagner beaucoup d'argent?

1970 va connaître un des plus importants
événements survenus dans l'histoire de la bonneterie :
le lancement de "8", première marque
conçue exclusivement pour la distribution moderne.
"8" va augmenter considérablement votre chiffre
d'affaires lingerie, car il correspond exactement à ce
qu'attendent vos clientes les plus intéressantes : les jeunes.

Slip et soutien-gorge coordonnés pour la première fois vendus dans la même boîte.

The 70s continued the ideal of thinness, it was PC to de-emphasise female shape again, but for overtly political reasons. Disenchantment with the lot of women brought the feminist cry 'Burn It,' in this the age of anorexia. Halter tops, string bikinis and bandeaux gave many normal sized girls serious emotional and social hang-ups about hanging down. Breastfeeding was less popular, but topless sunbathing was *de rigeuer* in Europe. Bralessness in general was a threat to the industry, so the 'no bra bra' was launched. Then the hard times returned and with it lingerie; slinky Janet Reger smalls and the Wonderbra overtook the heat-moulded bra and the cotton-knit 'natural' job.

above A French trade advertisment extolling the profit-making potential of the 1970s skin-fitting 'no bra bra'

right Vivienne Westwood's outside-underwear retro style bra-appeal demonstrated at its sexiest in 1991

far right Jean-Paul Gaultier's famous take on the 50s 'missile' bra as featured by Madonna in 1990

The 80s brought another swing towards equality, and Lycra heroically held the fort for us while we slugged it out in the boardroom in our power suits and Alaia. A brash flash said it all. In the locker room, Calvin Klein helped engender the concept of the female jock.

The avant-garde played games with the bra as outer wear, Jean Paul Gaultier placed it with pinstripe suits, a wry visual comment on the multiplicity of women's roles. Vivienne Westwood put retro style bras over street clothes and brought back the corset, much more tolerable at the end of the century, thanks to elastic and Lycra. Breastplates in metal and leather and Rifat Ozbek's bone example all made fleeting appearances in Vogue. Retailers like Victoria's Secret and La Perla made a killing in this decade because women, especially the Japanese, longed to wear something lacy and luxurious under their suit mufti.

In the 90s, much is made of the bra. It signifies girl power when depicted as a Wonderbra strap showing under a skimpy vest. It means one is attaining standards of personal best in choosing a sport bra in an advanced man-made fibre. It is knowing and motherly when voluptuously pushed up in a Vivienne Westwood Watteau dress and bawdy in a corset under a trouser suit. It is ballsy fun in Dolce and Gabbana jewelled corset or Versace safety-pin dress and it is practical, affordable chic when bought at Marks and Spencer. It is a sophisticated game re-living the 70s buying Glossies. It is pathetic when worn with a grass skirt in an Oxfam advert. It is scary when mentioned, but never seen as mastectomy wear. Today's conflicting images are as complex as they are numerous.

Why do we accept the Wonderbra ads 'or are you just pleased to see me' as 'just good fun' and yet the counterpart for mens' Brass Monkeys underwear be scrapped in the name of taste? As ever, the subtext is women's movement and sexuality. The area covered by the pants and bra marks out the erogenous zones and how far we go. In the 90s playing with big knickers or a 50s bra, we are stating the absence of off-limits areas. Maybe men haven't ever been oppressed by their underclothes, or come to the necessary self-awareness to joke about them.

Why do we perceive a woman wearing next to nothing in push-up bra and crop-top as powerful and invincible and not 'asking for it'? Why is so much emphasis placed on the folklore of the bra and its obvious correlation with a girl's ability to do or be anything she wants. It has always symbolised sexual power. Media messages show violence towards men who treat women badly or take them for granted. 'Ask before you borrow it', a slogan that really means it, and the French underwear company 'Malheur des hommes' (men's demise), show what that power means today.

Women have come a long way, as a saunter through any contemporary bra department shows; they are like museums these days. They can dress up in styles from past eras, without the discomfort of the whalebone and rationed fabrics, secure in the knowledge that there is no longer a particular size requirement for the 'in' look. We are due another bout of androgyny, but 'waist training' *a la* 19th Century and corsets are coming back, for the times when women want to be toyed with.

The reason we invent these funny little takes on retro styles and then move on, is because, as consumers, we can. But, if 'girl power' means that all a girl needs is a well-fitting bra and an attitude, the news is uplifting, but, where will that really take us?

the launch of vogue
magazine

Vogue began as a weekly gazette in 1892, backed by Gertrude Vanderbilt Whitney, a prominent society hostess and the daughter of shipping and railroad magnate Cornelius Vanderbilt. It was born into the New York of Edith Wharton, and published by and for people whose names were on the Social Register, the city's elite 'Four Hundred Families'. The Four Hundred, it was said, were all that could fit into Mrs Astor's ballroom at the same time. The magazine billed itself as the 'dignified authentic journal of society, fashion and the ceremonial side of life'.

However, that is not the *Vogue* we know and love. The key moment that established *Vogue* as the magazine it is today came in 1909 when an ambitious young publisher named Condé Nast took it over. He turned *Vogue* from being the organ of the élite into the bible of fashion. In the process, he changed the meaning of the word. Before 1909, 'vogue' meant foremost or prominent. Afterwards, it meant fashion itself.

The first publisher of **Vogue** was the wealthy Princetonian Arthur B. Turnure, who founded the exclusive Grolier Club and thought that publishing a chic little magazine for New York's burgeoning upper classes would be rather fun. Gertrude Vanderbilt Whitney, Alice Lippincott, Cornelius R. Cuyler, Mrs Stuyvesant Fish and other darlings of the dinner party circuit rushed to put their money in. The first issue appeared on 17 December 1892. By then, the magazine already had 250 shareholders and a list of annual subscribers, including the Astors, the Jays, the Van Rensselaers, the Stuyvesants, the Whitneys and the Vanderbilts.

Nast's background was very different from Turnure's or that of the readers of *Vogue*. Although he had been born in New York in 1878, he grew up in relative poverty in St Louis. His father came from a family of wealthy German Methodists. But he was the black sheep of the family as he had married a French Catholic and was cut off from the family funds. The young Nast attended Georgetown University, where he met and befriended Robert Collier. In 1898, Nast went on to study law at Washington University in St Louis. Meanwhile, Collier took over his father's dull-looking journal, *Collier's Weekly*, which then described itself as 'an illustrated journal of art, literature and current events'. Collier set about turning it into a new kind of magazine, mixing fiction with current events – lavishly illustrated with photographs of football and the Boer War, which was going on at the time. Back in St Louis, Nast had made a killing organising advertising and printing for exhibitors at the St Louis Exposition. Collier heard about this and thought that his friend's marketing talents should not go to waste in some law office. He offered Nast a job in New York. From 1900 to 1907, Nast was advertising manager, then business manager of *Collier's Weekly*. Nast's marketing genius carried it from last place to first place among the magazines that carried advertising. But that was not enough for the ambitious young Nast. In 1904, he became vice-president of the Home Pattern Company, which distributed paper dress patterns for the *Ladies' Home Journal* and a small society magazine called *Vogue*.

In 1905, Turnure died, leaving *Vogue* in the hands of his sister-in-law Marie Harrison. Although she was also *Vogue*'s editor, she had no clear idea where the magazine was going and opened negotiations with Nast. They dragged on, then eventually foundered.

above The founding father of *Vogue* as we know it, Condé Nast

previous page A startling image by Snowdon, then Anthony Armstrong-Jones, from Brtish *Vogue*, June 1957

right The very first *Vogue* cover dated 1892, when it was a weekly New York society gazette

VOGUE

VOGUE—A DEBUTANTE

In 1907, Nast quit *Collier's* to devote himself full-time to the Home Pattern Company. Under Nast, the company published the *Quarterly Style Book* and the *Monthly Style Book*, which Nast filled with advertising. They were fantastically profitable and Nast realised that you did not have to have a high circulation for a magazine to be successful. Advertisers would still be attracted if you targeted a specific market with special needs.

By 1909, the old *Vogue* was on its last legs. Its circulation had dropped to 14,000. Its advertising revenue was just $100,000, but it still reached some of the richest and most prominent members of New York society. So Nast bought it. He was just 36.

Unfortunately, Nast was saddled with Marie Harrison. Under the sales contract, she was to remain editor for five years. However, she had a very able young assistant named Edna Woolman Chase.

During the first six months, Nast did nothing, rarely even putting in an appearance at the office. Then quite suddenly, he became interested and cut the publication schedule back from once a week to once a fortnight and bumped up the cover price from 10 to 15 cents.

Other changes followed quickly – colour covers, more advertising, more *Vogue* patterns and more, much more, fashion. There was also a rapid turnover of staff as Nast hammered out the magazine's new formula. Dorothy Rothschild – better known later as Dorothy Parker – worked briefly for *Vogue*, before moving on to *Vanity Fair*, but not before writing the immortal caption: 'Brevity is the soul lingerie.'

The size of the issues climbed from just 30 pages when it was a weekly to 100 and over. However, the circulation remained modest – 30,000 in 1910, compared to *Ladies' Home Journal*'s 1,305,000.

However, in his relentless promotion of the magazine, Nast stressed that *Vogue* carried a great deal more advertising than any of its competitors – and that advertising did not come cheap. *Vogue* charged advertisers $10 per thousand readers, compared to *McCall's* magazine which charged $2. Nast claimed that *Vogue*'s low circulation cut out wastage. Advertisers in his magazine were reaching only those people who could afford to buy their products.

Worried by the success of *Vogue*, other women's magazine aped its formula, including more fashion and cutting back publication to twice monthly. But *Vogue* slowly built its circulation up to 100,000 – the optimum in Nast's philosophy – by keeping a clear vision of the role of magazine.

'*Vogue* is the technical advisor – the clothing specialist – to the woman of fashion in the matter of her clothes and personal adornment,' Nast said. First sketches and, later, photographs of the latest collections were

above Cover of the first edition of British *Vogue*, priced one shilling (5 pence), September 15th 1916

left A wonderful swimwear shot by George Hoyningen-Huené that appeared in British *Vogue*, June 1928

shipped back from Paris. *Vogue* also reported what fashionable Americans were wearing in Newport, Southampton, Tuxedo Park and Palm Beach. Another regular feature was what the English were wearing, particularly those who were titled as they were considered the height of fashion. Nast deliberately excluded fiction, fearing it would attract the indiscriminate audience of the mass-market publications.

But, despite considerable pressure from his staff, he retained the dress patterns which many considered to be infra dig in such a class conscious periodical, – the implication being that their readers could not afford the latest gown from Poiret or Vionnet if they dressed in homemade garments. However, Nast stood firm.

above The master photographer George Hoyningen-Huené in his studio with a copy of *Vogue* in 1928

right An outfit from the House of Worth pictured in British *Vogue* in 1935 by Horst P. Horst

'It is the avowed mission of *Vogue* to appeal not merely to women of great wealth, but more fundamentally, to women of taste,' he said in defence of his policy. 'A certain proportion of these readers will be found, necessarily, among the less well-to-do cousins of rich – women who not only belong rightfully to society, but who may in fact lead very fashionable lives, and, with their limited incomes, such women must look as well dressed as their affluent companions.'

Nast also knew that wealthy women liked to save money. President Theodore Roosevelt's wife told him that both she and her children wore clothes made up from *Vogue* patterns.

Although the circulation of *Vogue* remained comparatively small – it reached 141,000 in 1928 – profits skyrocketed. Eschewing the mass market and restricting the market was the formula for success. Other publishers caught on and the thousand of specialist magazines now on the newsagents' shelves are a direct result of Nast's publishing policy.

The success of *Vogue* led to disagreement between Nast and his editor Marie Harrison. With profits soaring, Harrison's sister, Arthur Turnure's widow Mrs Stimson, sued for 'lack of consideration', claiming essentially that she had been gypped by the sale. Nast hired a lawyer called MacDonald DeWitt to defend the suit, liked him and took him on staff. This was more than Marie Harrison could stand and she quit.

On 1 February 1914, Edna Woolman Chase took over. She had begun on Turnure's *Vogue* in the circulation department in 1895 at the age of 18 and went on to edit the magazine for 57 out of her 80 years. Ironically, she had been raised a Quaker by her grandparents in New Jersey and, consequently, should have taken no interest in fashion. 'Between us . . . we showed America the meaning of style', said Nast.

Chase was behind the setting up of *Le Syndicat de Défense de la Grande Couture Française* after the couturier Paul Poiret visited New York and saw pirated copies of his designs being sold in the shops at bargain-basement prices. When he arrived in Paris, Poiret explained to the other couturiers what he had seen and they threatened to boycott *Vogue*, which the couturiers held responsible for circulating details of their designs in the United States.

Vogue without Paris couture was unthinkable, so Chase, Nast and *Vogue*'s European representative Philippe Ortiz got together with Poiret and the other couturiers. The *Syndicat* was formed to prevent unlicensed copying of their designs. The couturiers knew they could not stop individual dressmakers making single copies, but together they could stop manufacturers mass producing their design with counterfeit labels. In 1935, Edna Chase was awarded the *Légion d'Honneur* for her services to the French fashion industry.

Chase was one of New York's legendary editors. A stickler for clarity, she argued that if she could not understand something, how could her readers be expected to? Her rejection letters made the toughest writers wilt and she demanded propriety at all times. After a young editor tried to commit suicide by throwing herself under a subway train, Chase remarked when the woman eventually returned to work: 'We at *Vogue* don't throw ourselves under subway trains, my dear. If we must, we take sleeping pills.'

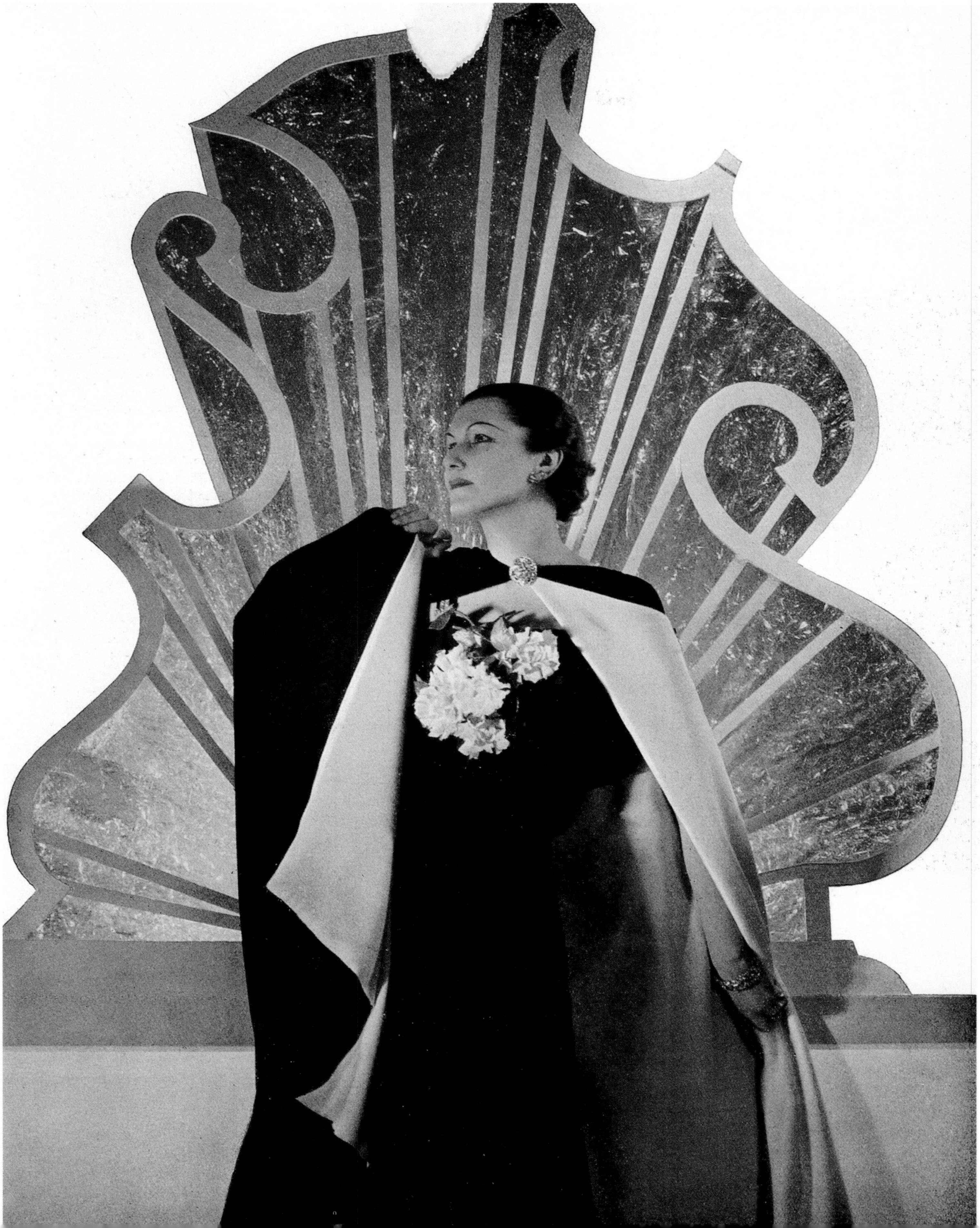

Chase got on well with her employer. They often ate together at a local Automat. Nevertheless, Chase made it clear that the editorial policy of the magazine was hers and hers alone. 'I cannot control the taste of our readers', she said, 'but I will not show editorially merchandise that I myself do not think is correct'.

During the Depression, Chase came under a great deal of pressure from the large department stores, such as Saks Fifth Avenue and Bergdorf Goodman, who spent a great deal of money advertising in *Vogue*. But Chase stood firm. 'As I see the function of *Vogue*, it is to produce a magazine of fashion, authority, information and beauty for our readers, and to make it as valuable a medium as possible in which advertisers may present their own messages to our readers', she said. 'We are responsible for the merchandise that we select from the shops and we are responsible for the manner in which we present it to our readers. We are equipped to do this work editorially, but we are not equipped in this capacity in the advertising department.'

Other than editorial procedure, Nast was in charge and he had a special employment policy which Chase, the hardworking Quaker, did not approve of. He paid Chase, fashion editor Carmel Snow and a team of five professional journalists a respectable sum to put the magazine out. Then he paid a pittance to hordes of debutante editors who drifted in and out of the magazine between social engagements. These socialites contributed little editorially, but they gave *Vogue* its high class tone. They also doubled as upper class models.

During World War I, the German submarine menace meant that *Vogue* was not reaching London, so British *Vogue* – known into insiders as Brogue – was launched in 1916. It was edited by Dorothy Todd, a friend of Virginia Woolf. Todd began to include experimental art and literary work. She was the first to show the work of Jean Cocteau in England and the first to publish Gertrude Stein's verse, turning British *Vogue* into a version of the American magazine *Vanity Fair*. What's more Todd was a lesbian. Edna Chase did not approve. The magazine began losing money – £25,000 a year. Nast sacked Todd in 1926 and brought Chase over. Chase edited the magazine throughout the General Strike (when it was hand delivered to the news-stands by the staff), until a new permanent editor could be found.

In 1920, French *Vogue* – or Frogue – was started. It lost money because the fashion houses did not need to advertise in France. They struck up exclusive deals with beautiful socialites, dressing them for next to nothing, provided they did not wear anything from any of the other houses. The first editor of the French edition of *Vogue* was a Chicagoan called Main Bocher. As Mainbocher, he went on to become a couturier. He was succeeded in 1929 by Michel de Brunhoff, but he spent more time on diplomatic missions to calm down the couture houses than actually editing the magazine. Despite the financial failure of French *Vogue*, it earned Nast his *Légion d'Honneur*.

A Spanish edition of the magazine made a brief appearance and German *Vogue* opened in 1928. It closed again in 1929, losing Nast $300,000 just before the Wall Street Crash. But the work of art editor Dr Mehemed Fehmy Agha impressed Nast so much that he brought him to New York where he became art director of American *Vogue*.

He was eventually succeeded by the great Alexander Liberman, who had been fired by Agha at the end of his first week on the magazine in 1941 because his layouts were not good enough. The following Monday, unbeknown to Dr Agha, Liberman had a meeting scheduled with Nast. Liberman turned up and they chatted about mutual acquaintances in Paris and Liberman showed Nast a Gold Medal diploma he had won for magazine production. 'A man like you must be on *Vogue*', said Nast.

'Dr Agha never said a word, I never said a word, and that's how I started on *Vogue*,' said Liberman. He went on to become editorial director of all the magazines.

The collapse of the stockmarket cost Nast dear. He lost many of his other publishing interests. But American, British and French *Vogue*s survived. These three magazines became a lucrative circuit for the great photographers of the era – Cecil Beaton, Baron Adolphe de Meyer, George Hoyningen-Huené, Erwin Blumenfeld, Horst P. Horst and Man Ray.

Of course, these photographers were freelance and it was not possible to hold on to them exclusively. During the 20s and 30s, American newspaper magnate William Randolph Hearst tried to knock *Vogue* off its perch with *Harper's Bazaar*. Hearst doubled what *Vogue* paid to anyone who would come and work for him. Edna Chase turned down Hearst's extravagant offer, but Heyworth Campbell, the founding art director of Nast's new-look *Vogue*, turned up at *Harper's*. So did *Vogue* fashion editor Carmel Snow, who became editor of Hearst's revamped *Harper's Bazaar*. Snow was a worthy adversary to Chase, but *Harper's* never quite caught up *Vogue* in circulation or advertising revenue.

Condé Nast died in 1942, but *Vogue* continued to be the home of some of the most innovative photographers of the age. After the war, the New Look brought with it new *Vogue* photographers – Irving Penn, Antony Armstrong-Jones (later Lord Snowdon), Norman Parkinson and Louis Faurer. And the fashion revolution that happened in the 60s was led by *Vogue* photographers who have now become household names – David Bailey, Terence Donovan, Richard Avedon and Helmut Newton.

Vogue continues to be the home of beautiful models, couture clothing and great photography. It is what all other fashion magazines strive to be. Since 1909, when Condé Nast took charge, to the present day, *Vogue* has remained synonymous with fashion.

right From British *Vogue*, May 1935, film legend Marlene Dietrich in a dress by Travis Banton of Hollywood, photographed by Edward Steichen

right From American *Vogue* in June 1948, a Cecil Beaton tableau scene featuring dresses by Charles James

4

chanel and sunbathing

previous page A postcard of the crowded beach at Juan les Pins on the French Riviera in the 1920s

left Gabrielle 'Coco' Chanel, here pictured in an archetypal casual suit in Paris in 1929

It's 1918 and the influential Gabrielle Chanel lies soaking up the sun's rays; a revolutionary pastime in a world where no one but peasants have a tan. At the time suntanned skin was a sign of having to work outdoors, of manual labour and poverty. Street traders, peasants and farm workers were marked with darkened hands and faces while the privileged ensured that their complexions remained pale in contrast; untouched by the sun and therefore unsullied by work and labour.

This had been the case through history so when Chanel lay out looking to get a tan in 1918 she was not just challenging the current beauty ideal, she was challenging the whole of social physical identity. This was not Chanel's only challenge to fashion and beauty of the time, but it was certainly the most difficult for people to accept.

In the pre-War years Chanel had spent summers at her store in the French seaside resort of Deauville, developing a new softer dress code for women who were still trussed up in severe corsets, raised collars and full length skirts. A big sports fan (attending race meetings in an eccentric looking masculine style) Chanel borrowed the soft jersey fabrics of the track and field and cut slouchy wrap cardigans and sailor neck blouses over gently pleated skirts that revealed the ankle. It was a completely new look and was slow to catch on, but eventually the ladies on the beach replaced their claustrophobic dress with this new relaxed fashion. In 1914 as a confirmation of the fashion revolution for women having begun, Chanel cut the first bathing costume for women and the sea was no longer reserved for men and small children. She was keen to show that women could be physical, active and strong and her next move was to encourage women to take on a healthy glow and to reflect this freedom in dress code in a new relaxed attitude to beauty.

Ironically, she was cautious in her first approach to suntanning, and in 1918 can be seen wearing gloves while sunning her face, so that her hands did not look like darkened labourer's hands. Her caution was reflective of the time it would take for tanning to become totally acceptable.

It was not until the depression of the War years was well and truly behind people that the innovations and ideas of Gabrielle Chanel started to gain momentum in society. The early 20s brought with them a *joie de vivre* and energy all of their own and Chanel's vision of vital beauty fitted perfectly into the zeitgeist. By 1923 women were sunbathing – with a healthy glow complementing a more unstructured approach to beauty routines and dress code; and with physical activities such as swimming becoming popular. The corset was abandoned in favour of looser, more comfortable undergarments and fashion's silhouette became short and fluid. With legs and arms bared, heavy maquillage looked inappropriate. A more natural look was required to complement the softly sunkissed body that was slowly being revealed after centuries of cover. Chanel had pre-empted the mood of the moment by about ten years.

The whole of history and its prejudices against sun-darkened skin had been reversed and suddenly a tan became associated with health and vitality, with an affluent lifestyle and with leisurely pursuits. Swimming and spa culture became popular amongst the rich, and exposed expanses of skin never previously seen in public.

The fashions of the 1920s and 30s reflected the new emphasis on the body and by the 30s the focus was such that a lithesome, athletic, almost Grecian ideal of beauty had emerged with an allover healthy glow and a well toned physique. Olympian, statuesque mannequins appeared in fashion images with hairstyles and maquillage that (in their minimalism) emphasised this attention to the skin and its good health. The work of photographers such as Hoynigen Heune perfectly exemplifies the focus on the body and the serene spa atmosphere that was so influential in the 30s. Statuesque poses, muscular limbs and sporty swimsuits all featured on models whose polished skin was sun slicked from outdoor pursuits. Sun worship was in fashion as part of a new classical ideal.

Whether or not it was the 2nd World War years (and its associated rationing, plain living and sobriety) that did it, 1948 certainly saw a brand

right From American *Vogue* in July 1930, an evocative swimwear shot by George Hoyningen-Huené

top The famous 'Don't be a Paleface' ad for Coppertone

above Brigitte Bardot in *And God Created Woman*, promoting beach nudity as much as the bikini

New Look in fashion, which suddenly reverted to heavily dressed hair, bold make up and even corset-like undergarments. Christian Dior's New Look embraced post-War excess with an extravagant silhouette that faintly resembled that of a turn of the century lady. And a sun tan was not part of the finished picture. Alabaster skin offset painted lips, and with only the ankle and the wrist on show the defining image was that of a fragile creature whose clothing did not necessarily protect her but certainly kept the sun at bay. Meanwhile a more enduring beauty ideal for the 20th Century was in the making on the other side of the Atlantic. Hollywood was booming and the starlet factory was in business.

Betty Grable in a spotty swimsuit sporting a perky tan and a cheeky grin was the popular face of post-War excess. Cinema was a major growth industry, and here were its new heroines; young pin-ups straight off the beach in fancy bathing costumes. The influence was global and although Chanel had created swimwear for women some 40 years earlier, beachwear really came into its own via the movies.

The functional almost athletic costumes of the 20s and 30s suddenly looked old fashioned and dull in a world that was fast becoming obsessed with popular culture. New costumes were inspired by showgirl style and Hollywood wardrobe - all filtered down into a new summer holiday wardrobe. From provincial seaside towns in England to America's major resorts the message was clear that glamour had hit the beach and everyone could take part. In sunglasses and a ruched one piece every woman could now get a tan in style.

Beaches everywhere became the boldest manifestation of cultural revolution with funfairs, holiday camps, rock'n'roll and the latest swimwear all transforming the traditional seaside outlook into one imbued by the new pop culture. And the effect was dramatized by the sheer numbers of people involved as everyone in the buoyant economic climate could afford to take part.

The growth during this time in mainstream tanning led to the promotion of various suncare products. Coppertone's advertising logo of a small girl and puppy pulling back her beach shorts to reveal a tan line is one the oldest and most enduring (and was later to be modelled by a very young Jodie Foster).

Previously unexposed expanses of flesh were now on show and the suntan had certainly moved on since Gabrielle Chanel's daring attempt at facial tanning in 1918.

The boundaries of acceptability were pushed even further in trying to achieve an all over tan, and as the 60s approached maximum tan potential was achieved – via the bikini.

While the 40s and 50s were all about the starlet style of Hollywood's pinups with their soft California girl suntans and fluffy hair, the 60s brought with them a more dramatic beauty ideal – that of the Mediterranean beach babe. Brigitte Bardot in a tiny bikini promoting *And God Created Woman* was the look of the future as the darker tan of life on the French and Italian Rivieras became fashionable. BB, Sophia Loren and Gina Lollobrigida were cinema's new sultry sex-appeal stars, and suddenly the desired tan deepened to dark bronze complemented by sunbleached, tousled hair.

above Roger Moore as James Bond in *The Man With The Golden Gun*, with classsic 70s Bond girls Maud Adams (left) and Britt Ekland

Hollywood took note and soon every starlet had adopted the look – including Ursula Andress whose emergence Amazon-like from the sea in the first James Bond movie *Dr No*, bronzed and bikini-ed, provided a defining image for the decade.

Aside from some brief, high fashion forays into the promotion of waif like pre-Raphaelite inspired pale complexions, the darker tan continued to deepen into the 70s to sub-continental levels. James Bond girls from around the globe sported the most intense tans yet and the bikini went micro, reflecting post 60s feminine liberation. Photographers such as Hans Feurer became known for their swimwear fashion plates that featured girls with tans so deep and glossy that they looked exotic.

Suncare products swamped the marketplace and promoted deep, rapid tanning with colour-enhancing lotions and ray-attracting oils literally scorching the skin to an authentic olive tone.

By the 80s a deep tan was a pre-requisite in looking attractive, and its association with the idea of affluent lifestyle, of being well travelled and of good health had, if anything, strengthened. Fake tan systems, sun beds and even self-tan tablets ensured that even the pale at heart could be well bronzed. However the dangers of the sun that are now so well known were just beginning to be understood. The 80s were full of images of deep olive tans, of sun lightened hair and of newly accessible tropical beaches. But towards the end of the decade the risks of skin cancer associated with sun exposure were being promoted and safe tanning suddenly had to become a focus for the skincare industry. Lotions and potions became preventative, yet irresponsible images of tanning continued to prevail in the media. It was not until the 90s that the media realised its responsibilities in promoting sensible images of tanning.

The acceptable fashion plate of the late 90s features a gently tanned image of beauty but the cultural change is a difficult one for people to adjust to. Safe tanning is still not practised by everyone and sunkissed skin continues to flatter and to sell dreams. Directional fashion has been saying that it is good to be pale since 1990, with a new wave of photographers and models promoting an offbeat vision of beauty in magazines such as *The Face*. Some of the earliest images such as Corrine Day's photographs of Kate Moss on the beach in Borneo in 1990 offered a stark contrast to the beauty convention yet the trend has gained little mainstream momentum.

Chanel's legacy will live on into the next century. The 20th Century will be recorded as the century with a tan and the 21st Century will act as a contrast – with exposure to the sun already becoming increasingly dangerous, and a return to pale skin as a beauty ideal slowly approaching.

above Published in *Elle* magazine in 1984, a swimwear shot by the Swiss photographer Hans Feurer

left From *Nova*, May/June 1969, beachwear details by photographer Giacobetti of a bikini by Baltrik

women in
trousers

5

In 1914 World War 1 broke out and this put women of all social classes into trousers. For most women, the freedom of movement that trousers offered was a totally new experience. In fact it could be said that The First World War was responsible for finally changing some outdated ideas about women wearing trousers.

Conventions in Western society had evolved over the centuries, defining a woman's role in the world, and how she should appear in public. For most of the 19th century women wore floor length dresses, severely corseted at the waist and supported by a crinoline. While men wore practical trousers and trouser suits, women were forced to struggle into these totally impractical fashions.

The earliest attempt by women to wear any form of trousers took place in America in 1849 when Amelia Jenks Bloomer launched the Rational Dress Campaign and appeared in ankle length knickerbockers. She wore these Cossack-style trousers with a short loose overskirt as a concession to convention and advocated this sensible costume in her own feminist paper *The Lily,* calling for functional clothing for women. The Bloomer costume reached Britain in 1851, but never really caught on. Whenever it was worn in public 'The Bloomer' inspired outrage or amusement, and most women were not yet confident enough to cope with the ridicule.

The Bloomer costume briefly fell out of fashion only to make a strong come-back during the 1880s. By this time women were starting to voice their opinions about society's inequalities and taking action by initiating liberating changes in their lives. One change was participation in outdoor sports and leisure activities, particularly bicycling.

Cycling illustrated how impractical bustles and crinolines were for the active woman, hence Bloomers were reintroduced as a suitable attire. This enabled the bicycle to become an important symbol of young women's independence, especially as it relieved them of their chaperones!

By the turn of the century a 'new woman' had emerged. Mrs Pankhurst and her fellow suffragettes had begun their Campaign for Votes for Women, and more and more young women were now entering universities. It was the dawn of the career girl whose attitudes were embodied in the 'modern' suit she wore, which was less fussy and constrictive than the previous Victorian fashions. Most significantly, it was tailored like a man's suit, which gave young women a look of efficiency that was respected by their male employers, and enabled them to finally begin participating in the man's world.

It wasn't until a revolutionary fashion designer, Paul Poiret, launched his exciting new designs in 1910 that female trousers were considered a possibility. Poiret took inspiration from the Far East where for centuries women had been allowed freedom of movement in loose pyjama style outfits. He was undoubtedly inspired by the exotic Ballets Russes presented by Serge Diaghilev in Paris in 1909. Some of Poiret's designs featured brocade or embroidered tunics worn over baggy harem trousers.

They were loose and voluminous, moving away from the prevailing mature look towards a much younger style. In 1911 he advertised these outfits as a 'fashion of tomorrow', but they were too avant garde for most tastes and were worn only by high society, the fashion conscious and aspiring 'bohemians'.

previous page From a 60s ad, not for a unisex outfit but a man's suit – but still a sign of the times

right A portrait of Amelia Bloomer which appeared on the sheet music for 'The Bloomer Polka' in 1850

The Girl on the Land
Serves the Nation's Need

apply Y.W.C.A
Land Service Committe

With most men enlisted into the armed services, in 1915 women were called upon to help in the war effort. Those that went to work in factories to produce shells, bombs and tanks were known as munitions workers. As part of their protective clothing, munitions workers were issued with either men's overalls, which were belted tunics over loose trousers, or men's boiler suits. Some women went to work as agricultural labourers or 'land girls', where they wore knee-breeches tucked into thick socks. Others worked for the railways, tramways, bus companies or postal services where they were also given the option of wearing trousers. Between 1914 and 1918 it had become quite common to see women wearing some form of trousers. But despite this big leap for female emancipation it didn't automatically lead to women donning trousers in civilian life.

Poiret's pantaloons or harem trousers designed for women before the war had a limited following, but by the early 1920s designers were suggesting Turkish trouser suits or pyjamas for wear at home in the evening as 'hostess' or 'lounging' pyjamas.

The 1920s also marked the beginning of the cult of the open air. Sun bathing was promoted as healthy, and influential people like Coco Chanel were making the suntan fashionable. Society belles and the wealthy flocked to the Riviera to see and be seen. The beaches in the South of France allowed an informality that encouraged casual fashion, and flouted dress code conventions. As an advocate of outdoor living Coco Chanel encouraged women to wear loose baggy trouser length pants or beach pyjamas. These proved to be very popular with women as they were comfortable and allowed women to be athletic and participate in active beach sports. The pyjamas were made with fluid and feminine lightweight fabrics. They were also flattering to the female form as they emphasised a woman's limbs, making her appear sleek and lithe.

By the late 20s men were gradually becoming more accustomed to the sight of young women in these leisure pyjamas, either at fashionable resorts or in the magazine society pages. It was only when women started wearing more mannish and tailored trousers as everyday wear that opinions for and against became more polarised.

During 1927 several female tennis stars began wearing men's trousers on the court. This didn't catch on, but masculine styling did. Some women took to flaunting their emancipation to an extreme, and openly contradicted social conventions by adapting an entirely male look. They wore tailored men's suits with trousers or plus fours and even cut their hair shorter than a bob, into what became known as an Eton crop. They also assumed a more robust manner, and even smoked cigars. This behaviour was deemed preposterous and unladylike, and was often ridiculed in sketches in *Punch* and other satirical magazines.

Ironically the earliest examples of women cross-dressing as men had in fact been as satire. As early as the 1660s during the Restoration period women had appeared in theatrical comedies dressed as men in parts known as the 'breeches' role. This evolved into the 'Principal Boy' role in pantomime by the 19th Century. Before the 1920s the stage had been the only place that a woman's legs could be seen in public.

left A First World War 'land girls'
poster by the artist Edward Penfield
and published by the Y.W.C.A.

above   A publicity shot of 30s actress Marlene Dietrich wearing her archetypal man's suit

right   Navy-inspired bell-bottom women's trousers as holiday wear, from French *Vogue* magazine, 1931

far right   A WAAF (the Women's Auxiliary Air Force) on parade at an RAF dog-training school, UK 1946

In 1928 women finally secured the right to vote, but they had already shown that they could wear the trousers. For many women, to dress like a man in public was the ultimate in liberation. This mannish look was epitomised by Marlene Dietrich who would often be photographed both on and off screen wearing a man's suit with trousers, a boyish cap and striking a male pose with a cigarette. In her 1930 film *Morocco* she wore a man's tuxedo. Like many Hollywood stars she helped set a fashion trend, if only in the independent confidence she exuded. Views about social conventions were quickly changing, and by the mid 30s a major change in women's fashion had taken place.

No longer confined to holiday resorts and evening soirees, leisure pyjamas evolved. They became more tailored in heavier fabrics with pleats, pockets and creases much closer to the man's style of trouser and were known as slacks. This heralded the real arrival of women's trousers.

It wasn't long before women in slacks were a frequent feature in *Vogue* magazine. Particularly the new breed of female aviators. They were portrayed as the ultimate emancipated woman, confident, independent and part of the automotive age. The plane and car was now the equivalent of the woman's bicycle of the 1880s. Women were photographed wearing slacks or flying suits next to the planes they flew single handedly. *Vogue* readers of the 1930s wanted to know what these women wore, and trousers were the fashion.

Ironically, by the end of the 30s images of female aviators were a common sight, but it wasn't for setting new records. The Second World War had started and once again women were called upon to help. This time they also were being recruited for active service. Women's divisions of the air force and navy had already been established, as the WAAF and the WRNS. Women's military uniforms now included trousers, which had a noticeable effect on civilian fashions, which acquired a utilitarian look. Trousers were practical and consequently more women were encouraged to wear them in civilian life. They provided a warm alternative to stockings which were no longer obtainable during the war, and were comfortable for the long periods sitting in air raid shelters. The Siren-Suit, styled from a man's boiler suit, was an outfit specially designed for women and children to wear in air raid shelters.

Once the war had ended women returned to wearing primarily dresses and skirts – by choice! Most women had had enough of utilitarian trousers and siren suits. They wanted to look glamorous again! Christian Dior was well aware of this when he launched his New Look in 1947. The feeling of austerity had not affected America however, especially not on the West Coast. While Europe suffered from the after effects of the war, California was setting the new trends in leisurewear; casual clothes for the increasingly popular outdoor recreations. It was also in America where the new teenage lifestyle was developing, a consumerism driven by the under-20s which eventually became identified as 'youth culture'.

College kids would meet up at their local soda fountain to socialise and listen to the jukebox, or go down to the beach in their hot-rods to 'hang out' and have a clam-bake. Girls wanted to have as much fun as the boys. They discovered that the ideal clothing for their lifestyle was denim jeans. Denim jeans had been invented by an emigre from Bavaria named Levi Strauss who had come to America in 1850 to join the gold rush. It was then that he made his first pair of jeans, primarily as a tough and durable work trouser for men.

In America by the mid-40s girls had started wearing jeans, which were frowned upon for making the girls appear less lady-like, and hence got the girls labelled as 'tom-boys'. Girls adapted their jeans to suit their active lifestyles, and rolled them up to just below the knee for easy bicycle riding.

The early 1950s saw elements of American youth culture beginning to influence teenagers in Britain. Girls had their own ideas about fashion, and invented unique styles based on a mixture of 'borrowed' cultures. The immigration of Italians to Britain after the War was one factor leading to a more cosmpolitan society, a feature of which was the fad for Italian-style espresso coffee bars. These became the popular meeting places for teenage girls to compare fashion ideas, creating a look that was a distinct blend of American casual and Continental chic.

The new style of trousers for girls in the 1950s were very fitted around the hips and bottom, and tapered, parallel to the leg, down to the ankle. Which variation of this basic style was 'in' determined how short the trouser leg was cut. 'Pedal pushers' were cut short at the knee, or just below, and often ended with a neatly folded cuff. They primarily served to make cycling easier. In Britain and on the Continent girls adapted them for riding on the back of scooters. 'Capri pants' were a longer ¾ length trouser that finished at the calf with small slits on either side. Girls wore both styles with sweaters, T-shirts or artists smocks, short socks and pumps. This was a simple understated look that came to be epitomised by chic Hollywood stars such as Audrey Hepburn.

Advertising was quick to adopt these new images of women in their campaigns, where women dressed in the new casual fashions happily demonstrated home appliances. It was part of the futuristic image of the 50s where housework was no longer presented as a chore, but as recreation.

Slimma go colour in their co-ordinated Total Look

Slimma Limited,
13/14 Woodstock Street,
London, W.1.

right A British ad from the 1960s for women's slacks, featuring in the front the top model of the day Twiggy

far right From the 60s British TV show *The Avengers*, actress Diana Rigg in karate mode as Emma Peel

New post-war synthetic and elasticated fabrics, initially developed for ski-wear meant that women's trousers could be tight, but stretchy and non-restrictive. These casual 'play' trousers could be produced in exciting new patterns like tartan and leopard print. Girls paired these with tight sweaters and gypsy-style hoop earrings to mimic the 'cool' Italian look that was all the rage.

From this point onwards, designers regularly introduced new and inventive trouser styles. The most significant trouser trend during the 1960s was the trouser suit. This was a two-piece garment which combined a tunic or jacket with trousers of matching fabric. It is widely believed that the success of the trouser suit in the 60s was actually a reaction against the miniskirt and suggested a return of the 'mannish' look that had flourished during the 30s.

Trouser suits with tunics had a minimalist simplicity, especially when produced in bold white or subtle pastel shades suggesting an outfit for the 21st Century. Designers like Andre Courreges and Pierre Cardin drew inspiration from the space-age 60s and Bridget Riley's 'Op Art' to create an exciting new look for women. The trouser suit offered women a versatile look for all occasions, day or night.

The cat-suit was another big development in women's fashion during the 60s. Derived from the flying-suit, the cat-suit was made in stretch Crimplenes or Jersey to create a figure-hugging zip-up all-in-one. They were popularised by a TV programme of the mid-60s called *The Avengers* featuring the archetypal Emma Peel. She represented the new dynamic ultra-modern woman of the 20th Century. Her avant garde clothes were designed by John Bates of Jean Varon who was also inspired by the 'futuristic' look of the times. His famous 'Emmapeelers' as he called them, were very minimal outfits in only one colour with a thin stripe or chain link belt for adornment. Bates also designed trouser suits made of PVC or leather for Miss Peel, which were thought to be very risqué and kinky, the latter a key word in the swinging 60s.

Now well established, women's trousers were part of every fashion designers collection. This led to an explosion of trouser styles that made use of every conceivable natural or synthetic fabric available, including 'see-through' materials. With this flood of diverse trouser styles now available for women an interesting phenomenon occurred: 'unisex' fashion. Unisex boutiques opened up as one-stop shops to cater for both boys and girls. The most popular styles for both sexes were denim, satin, or leather suits which consisted of tight jeans that flared out from the knee, with a matching fabric waistcoat and jacket. As men had started to grow their hair longer, it was no longer a case of women looking like men, but men looking like women.

This affinity continued into the early 70s. It was not just a similar appearance, but also similar ideals. By 1967 many young men and women 'dropped out' and became hippies, looking to the East for spiritual enlightenment. Clothes were brought back, or imported, from India and

Morocco, influencing home grown fashion. Flared trousers were made of plain or crushed velvet and Denim jeans were embroidered with flowers and mythical creatures. Hippies experimented with drugs, and their hallucinogenic 'trips' were translated into crazy swirling multi-coloured patterns. Their beliefs inspired a fashion trend for both sexes .

By the mid-70s women had discovered that wearing trousers gave them a hidden cloak of neutrality that removed their sexuality and allowed them to compete more effectively in the male dominated workplace. The 1900s career girl was now an executive that went on business lunches and held boardroom meetings. She was extremely confident and was more independent and liberated than ever. Designers created outfits specifically for these women. Pinstripe business suits based on the city gent style complete with trousers and waistcoats were modelled by strident long legged models like Jerry Hall and Verushka who helped create the look and attitude used in the 70s advertising campaign for Charlie perfume. Denim jeans were re-designed to specifically fit a woman's shape, and the designer's name on a visible label became all important, now known as 'designer' jeans. This period launched 'power dressing' and the influence of Italian fashion design.

The high flying businesswoman went hand in hand with another trend that originated in America: the health craze. Jogging, dance classes and aerobics were part of the fitness fixation which caught on in Britain by the 1980s. This led to a boom in the sports and leisure wear industry as more and more women vied for the most fashionable outfit in the gym. Jogging outfits proved to be so comfortable that men and women adapted them for everyday clothes, replacing their previous casualwear.

By the mid-80s black 'rap' artists adopted sportswear as their street style uniform. Brand and team name sports tops, caps, sweat pants, jeans and trainers became part of the identity. All-girl rap acts followed suit, and through their popularity in the charts created a sportswear fashion trend that rivals the denim jean as the top casual look today.

Women in trousers have always reflected social change, and growing confidence in women and their place in society. This was especially true during the 70s when Vivienne Westwood and Malcolm McLaren opened their shop SEX. Their original collections started as anarchic anti-fashion reactions to the industry. Years later their rubber, leather and PVC fetishistic and fantasy clothes inspired mainstream fashion. Women were no longer inhibited or self conscious about wearing tight wet look PVC trousers in the high street.

Now every woman has a pair of trousers of some kind in her wardrobe, whether part of an Armani suit, or a pair of ripped and faded denim jeans. The trouser fashions of the 1990s have seen many reinterpretations of retro-styles, such as flares and bell bottoms, or as in the collections of the last two years which looked back to the 50s, featuring pedal pushers and capri pants. And on the street, girls have adopted a more masculine look by wearing army combat trousers with trainers or Dr Marten boots. It's a hybrid style of punk, hippie and sportswear casual that continues to illustrate women's increasing sense of equality and freedom of choice in society, of which women in trousers have been a constant measure.

right   Unisex dressing from 1969 with identical trouser suits for both men and women

far right   Power dressing for the 90s with a no-nonsense catwalk suit from Ralph Lauren

man ray –
fashion
photography
as art

Before Man Ray, there was no such thing as a fashion photographer. And although Man Ray was one of the people who created the discipline, he himself never worked at it full time. Photography was just one of the ways he paid the rent while he was establishing himself as an avant garde artist. So when Condé Nast asked him to supply fashion shots for the inaugural issue of French *Vogue*, it was a bit like delivering Naomi Campbell into the hands of Damien Hirst.

Man Ray was notorious in Paris before he arrived there in 1921. Born Enamel Rabinovitch in Philadelphia, 1890, his family moved to Brooklyn, New York, in 1897. At 15, he changed his name to Man Ray, which was how he was known for the rest of his life. At 18, he began work as a draftsman and designer, studying art at night. By the time he was 22, he was designing the covers for Emma Goldman's anarchist magazine *Mother Earth*.

In 1914, he moved out to an artist's colony in New Jersey where he met the artist Marcel Duchamp. The following year, Man Ray had his first one-man exhibition in New York and began taking photographs to reproduce his paintings for the catalogue. He also published photographs in the avant garde journal *391* and in the sole issue of *New York Dada*.

At his second one-man exhibition, he outraged the art world by displaying paintings made with a spray gun. Under the influence of Duchamp and Francis Picabia, he began developing the art of provocation. Before he left for France in 1921, he became interested in what he called 'ready-mades', commercially manufactured objects that he exhibited as works of art. The most famous was *Le Cadeau* (The Gift). It was a flat iron with a line of tacks glued to the bottom, rendering it useless. It has become one of the enduring images of the century.

The burgeoning avant garde art world of Paris greeted Man Ray with open arms. But he needed to make a living, so he began taking pictures of the famous people he was introduced to. His sitters included Pablo Picasso, Sinclair Lewis, Henri Matisse, Gertrude Stein and James Joyce. Joyce even used Ray's portrait to publicise his new book *Ulysses*. But for Man Ray even portraiture was not a straightforward business. He gave one sitter three pairs of eyes. In 1924, he also produced the famous image *Le Violin d'Ingres*, a female nude with the f-holes of a violin superimposed photographically on her back.

As well as making money with his photography, Man Ray explored its possibilities as an art form. He experimented with solarisation, a process by which part of the image is made positive, part negative made by exposing the film to a flash of light during developing. It was first used in 1840, but Man Ray developed its uses as an aesthetic effect. He also rediscovered cameraless photography making what he called 'Rayographs', where objects were put directly on the photographic plate and exposed. He published a book of them called *Les Champs Délicieux* (The Delightful Fields) in 1922.

Man Ray continued making 'ready-mades'. In 1923, he made *Object to be Destroyed*, a metronome with a photograph of an eye stuck to the pendulum. Again it became one of the most famous images of the 20th Century, and Man Ray's wish came true in 1957, when it was destroyed by anti-Dada rioters.

He also made a number of films, usually in collaboration with Marcel Duchamp. In one, *Le Retour à la Raison* (The Return to Reason, 1923), he applied his Rayograph technique to motion pictures.

Through Gabrielle, the first wife of Francis Picabia, Man Ray met the couturier Paul Poiret and began taking photographs for him. Poiret was a collector of avant garde art and Man Ray realised that Poiret required something original, something quite different from conventional commercial fashion pictures. Man Ray came up with a new formula. It was simply: 'Line, colour, texture and, above all, sex appeal.'

One of his earliest fashion shots shows a model wearing a peacock-tailed dress designed by Poiret posed alongside a modernist sculpture by Constantin Brancusi. Man Ray brought together fashion, art and the sex appeal of a beautiful woman in one picture.

Man Ray also began taking the society pictures so much in demand by the new fashion magazines. At the Comte Etienne de Beaumont's costume ball in June 1924, he captured Picasso dressed as a toreador, Nancy Cunard in a brocade trouser suit and Sara and Gerald Murphy's silk versions of cubist paintings. And at the Futurists' ball, he photographed Marie-Laure, wife of the host the Vicomte de Noailles, dressed as a giant squid.

The zenith of his work as a society photographer was his shots of the Comtesse Pecci-Blunt's Bal Blanc where everyone was dressed in white, which he covered for *Vogue* in 1930. With his assistant Lee Miller, Man Ray had a hand-coloured film made by pioneer French film-maker George Mélièis projected on the couples on the dancefloor.

But mostly Man Ray photographed his fellow Dadaists, who had taken to dressing in the out-moded clothes of the Belle Époque, with spats, canes, felt gloves and snap-brimmed fedoras. These were printed in magazine such as *Vu, Paris Magazine, Variétés, Jazz* and *L'Art Vivant*, which made their way back to the States. This had a double effect. It made both the Dadaists and their photographer famous.

He began working for *Vogue, Vanity Fair* and the in-house magazine *Charm* on fashion shoots, while his more experimental work was appearing in small artistic journals such as *Broom, Dial* and *The Little*

previous page Published in 1937 in *Harper's Bazaar*, entitled *Madness of the moment, Paquin's feather boa in all the colors of Harlem*

left A self-portrait from 1932, a print which was taken from Man Ray's original solarised negative

above Using his own painting *Observatory Time – The Lovers* as a background, Man Ray photographed a model in a Jacques Fath gown for *Observatory Time – Mode,* published in *Harper's Bazaar* in 1936

left Surrealist artist Oscar Dominguez created an upholstered wheelbarrow for Man Ray to photograph a model wearing a Lucien Lelong evening gown

Review. But he did not tailor his style to the client. One of the pictures commissioned by Condé Nast for the first issue of *Vogue* also appeared on the cover of the 25 July 1925 issue of *La Révolution Surréaliste,* with the caption: 'And war on work.' The picture showed a wooden mannequin in a couturier dress ascending a staircase.

Man Ray was not such a strange choice of photographer to feature in the inaugural issue of French *Vogue.* He was already getting lucrative commissions from British *Vogue* after taking a portrait of the editor Dorothy Todd. Then, in 1934, art director Alexey Brodovitch, who had recently been hired by editor Carmel Snow, introduced Man Ray to *Harper's Bazaar,* which began to take most of his output.

As Dada transmogrified into Surrealism, fashionable photographers such as Cecil Beaton, George Hoyningen-Huené and Horst P. Horst began to feature surrealist props like broken columns in their fashion pictures. Man Ray never did. He used plain backdrops and depended on light and movement for effects. However, he occasionally incorporated contemporary works of art – often his own or the work of Oscar Dominguez or Alberto Giacometti. Designers such as Coco Chanel and Elsa Schiaparelli, who Man Ray had known from his New York days, were avid collectors of modern art and like to stress their involvement in the latest artistic movements. Salvador Dali and Jean Cocteau collaborated with Schiaparelli on some of her more outrageous designs.

Man Ray, however, was not always very enthusiastic about this fusion of art and fashion.

'Extraordinary results were expected of me,' he said, 'but I soon discovered that editors were more interested in using my name than in a new idea or presentation.'

However, they often shied away from using his more far-fetched works. When they suggested a reduction in his fee, Man Ray demanded that they double his money to soothe his injured pride.

Instead of using static poses, Man Ray shot his studio sessions like a movie director. Modern fashion, Man Ray believed, had to be presented in a modern way. Often he would cut the head off the model in his pictures, or showed just parts of them. Jewellery and accessories were photographed on dismembered hands, and amorphous parts of the models' bodies were highlighted on mysterious, dark sets.

Man Ray's fashion shots were never simply portraits of the model. They never look out of the picture enticingly or defiantly. In fact, the women show no emotion at all. They are passive objects used only for the aesthetic of the couturier and photographer. In his many photographs of nudes for the art magazines, the models are also treated in the same dispassionate way.

However, Man Ray did some private work for William Seabrook, the travel writer and avowed misogynist. The models were often required to wear uncomfortable, if not painful, garments. There were explicit references to the work of the Marquis de Sade. The women were often tied up, their hands, breasts and lips photographed with an almost fetishistic appreciation. At that time, of course, these photographs were not suitable for publication, but he used the same meticulous approach to lighting and posing that appears in his fashion work.

But *Harper's Bazaar* gave him a relatively free hand to explore experimental techniques. He used Rayographs to illustrate sheer stockings

right Untitled c.1928-9. One of
Man Ray's notorious erotic studies
commissioned by William Seabrook

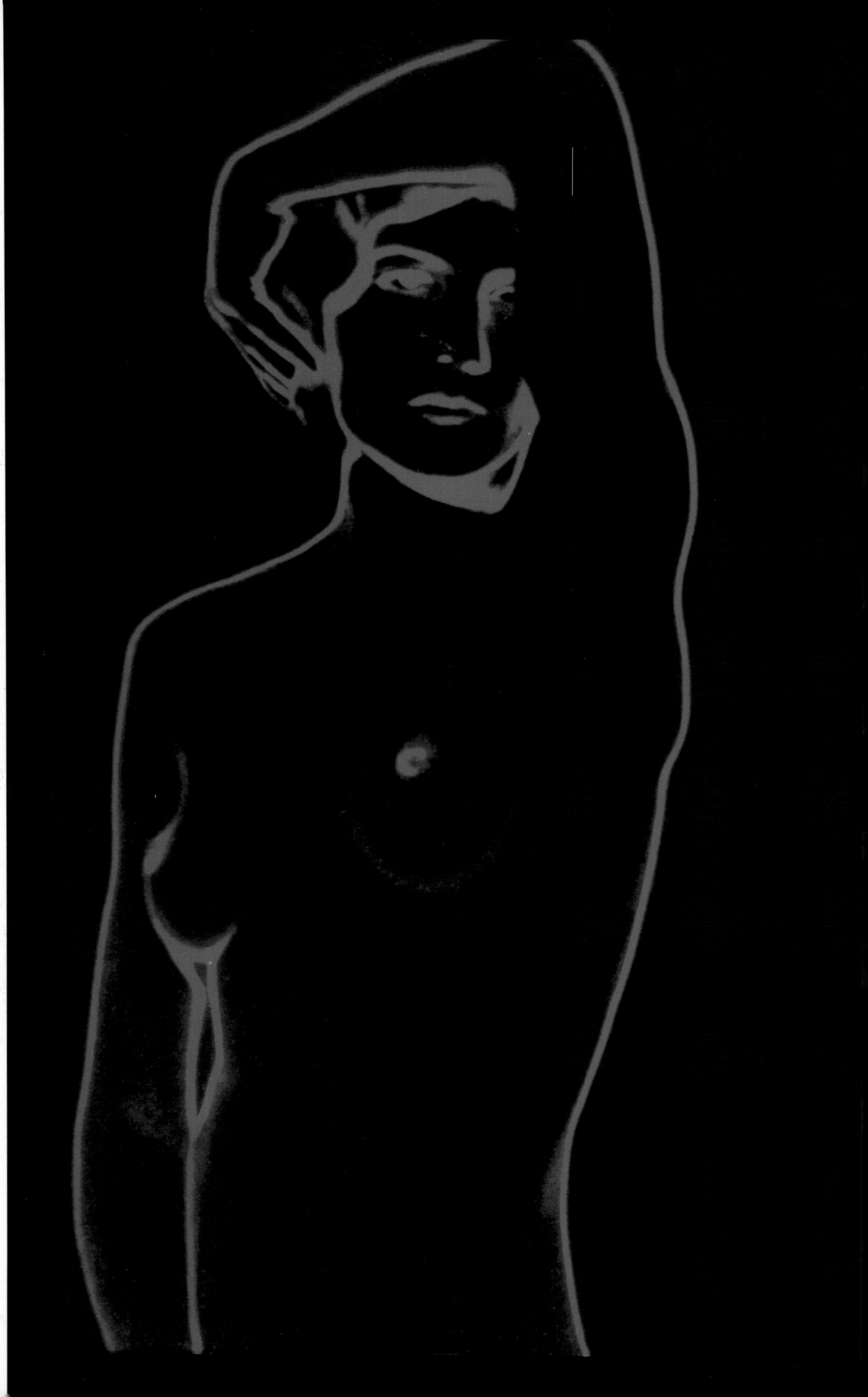

and in the picture *Fashion by Radio*, he used similar methods to create a wavy pattern showing fashion coming over the short-wave.

He used solarisation to make a picture called *This Young Grey Head,* which shows what an attractive young woman would look like with grey hair. And in *Beauty in Ultra-Violet,* solarisation is used to produce a halo of violet light around a nude torso.

With the onset of the Depression, the small magazines that published Ray's artistic work folded. This meant that Ray's work was not being seen back in America. So he took matters into his own hands and published *Photographs by Man Ray, 1920-34*. It was a collection of 105 portraits, nudes, Rayographs and solarisations, many of which would not have been out of place in the pages of *Harper's Bazaar*. But the accompanying text, in English, was written by the luminaries of Dada and Surrealism – Marcel Duchamp, Tristian Tzara, Paul Éluard and André Breton.

Nevertheless, Ray's reputation as a fashion photographer continued to eclipse his work as an artist. Major works, such as the painting *Observation Time – The Lovers* (1932-1934), were ignored. While the Depression meant that fellow artists were starving, Man Ray found he was making more money than ever. He wore Savile Row suits, drove the latest Voisin and bought a house in the country.

But he shared his good fortune with his friends and lovers when he could. Man Ray employed Nusch Éluard, wife of the poet Paul Éluard as a model and arranged for Éluard to review an exhibition of African hats. Man Ray's girlfriend Ady Fidelin modelled one of the hats for him. But that was the only time he was allowed to use her. She was a mulatto from Haiti and thought to be unsuitable to model couture clothes because she was black.

In 1936, with André Breton, he produced the pamphlet *Photography n'est pas l'art* (Photography Is Not Art). In it, Man Ray published his most artistic work – details of insects, abstract images, pictures of frogs mating. But he could not help including two of his fashion images. One is simply of a model in a sheer nightie, entitled *Le sex appeal*. The other shows a fruit tree, wrapped against the cold. It is captioned: *New Winter Fashions*. In the text, Breton and Man Ray argued that photography was not an art because it was so flexible and versatile, while art was narrow and rigid.

Man Ray continued his work as an artist, though. That year, he exhibited his artistic work in the International Surrealist Exhibition in London and in the show 'Fantastic Art, Dada, Surrealism' at the Museum of Modern Art in New York. But while he was in New York, he continued to fulfil numerous fashion assignments.

During the 1920s and early 1930s, the Dadaists and Surrealists had used magazines to make themselves famous and disseminate their ideas. But as the 1930s drew on, Ray's work began to be seen as purely commercial and, therefore, in the eyes of the artistic world, tainted. The power of the printed page had built Man Ray an international reputation as a fashion photographer, but as an artist he was neglected.

Dada and Surrealism soon came to be seen as a frivolity in the face of the advancing German army. Man Ray left Paris and returned to America, where he found himself in demand by the fashion magazines, but not by the art galleries. He turned the fashion magazines down flat and moved to

above *Le sex appeal*, 1936, from Man Ray's collaboration with André Breton *Photography n'est pas l'art*

left The remarkable *Beauty in Ultra Violet* in which the technique of solarisation was used stunningly

Hollywood where he concentrated on painting, though he did one last fashion shoot for *Harper's Bazaar* in 1942.

In 1946, Man Ray returned to France, and he remained in Paris for the rest of his life. He continued working mainly in paint, and although he did experiment with colour photography in the late 1950s and early 1960s, he was always very careful not to let his photographic work overshadow his serious work as an artist again.

In later life, he did manage to attain recognition as an artist as well as a photographer. He exhibited at the Institute of Contemporary Art in London in 1959, and in 1961 he was awarded a gold medal for photography at the Venice Biennale. The following year a major retrospective of his work was staged at the Bibilothèque Nationale in Paris. This exhibition also toured Europe ten years later.

Although the German Photographic Society gave him their cultural award in 1966, by the time Man Ray died in Paris in 1976, his artistic work had completely eclipsed his fashion photography. A huge exhibition of his work as an artist was mounted in the Pompidou Centre in Paris in 1982 and another one toured the US in 1988.

It was only in 1990, that an exhibition of Man Ray's fashion photography was mounted by the International Center of Photography in New York. It toured Europe and Asia.

Man Ray's importance as a fashion photographer lies in the fact that he brought the aesthetics of the artist into the commercial world. Art, particularly modern art, did not live in a world of its own, he maintained. A fashion photograph is primarily a picture. It should have a visual excitement beyond the garment that is being displayed.

Man Ray was primarily an image maker, in his artistic work, in his portraiture and in his fashion work. His Dada and Surrealist background made his pictures of an expensive couture dress somehow subversive. He took art and put it on the news-stands.

Photomechanical reproduction made culture a consumable like clothes or food. The reader could never be sure how much irony was intended. In his own surrealistic way, was he mocking the magazines he worked for, or selling out to them? The answer was a complex surrealistic paradox, which gave him money and fame, as well as the acclaim of his surrealist friends whose ideas he took to a wider audience.

During his time between the wars in Paris, Man Ray influenced all the photographers working in fashion. They too imported elements of high art into the pictures. After Man Ray, fashion photographers were no longer expected to purely take a picture of a piece of merchandise. The picture had to be a work of art as well. By association, that meant the creation of the couturier was a work of art too. The generations of fashion photographers who have followed Man Ray have learnt that lesson well. He gave them the freedom to be daring and inventive and Man Ray's legacy can be seen clearly in the fashion magazines of today.

right Part of a Chanel fashion shoot for *Harper's Bazaar* (September 1937) with background sculpture *Albatross* by Alberto Giacometti

schiaparelli
– humour and
surrealism

7

In 1927 the fashion world had just become used to the minimal styling and colour palettes brought about by Gabrielle Chanel; trousers on women were no longer shocking, comfortable sporty fabrications were much in use, and restrictive gravity-defying undergarments had been replaced by a liberating softness in silhouette. There was very little change in fashion until Elsa Schiaparelli suddenly introduced a new influence into dressing – that of the art world.

Elsa Schiaparelli, determined to make an impact in the Paris fashion world, arrived at the Ritz for a lunch in 1927 wearing a garment that she knew would create a stir. It was a simple black sweater knitted by an Armenian using an unusual traditional stitch that involved the use of three needles. The sweater was simple in style but at the neck it featured a *trompe l'oeil* white bow looking like a tied scarf. The novel, decorative treatment looked completely new and different and injected an element of humour into the room full of people wearing serious, minimalist fashionable clothing. This was a stunt to kick-start Schiaparelli's career with everyone at the lunch placing orders for copies (including an order for 40 pieces from Lord and Taylor in New York). But it also marked the start of a relationship between art and fashion, particularly with Surrealism.

Elsa Schiaparelli was born into a very wealthy Italian family and from an early age was surrounded by much to fire the imagination. Palazzo Corsini, her childhood home in Rome, was full of dramatic architectural features, frescoes and tapestries, and featured an exquisite historical library. The young Schiaparelli was intrigued by the images, omnipresent in the architecture and the library, of religion and astrology. She became immersed in books and pictures relating to the two subjects, and they remained major visual influences in her life's work.

As Elsa grew up she became interested in music and poetry and had concert reviews and a volume of poetry, entitled *Arethusa*, published by the age of 20. However, she was prevented from achieving any literary ambitions having been shunted around Europe for a number of years in a vain attempt by her parents to find her a suitable husband. Eventually she found a husband for herself and married without her parents consent in London in 1914. The newly wed Elsa Kerlor then spent three years living in New York with her husband. He travelled as a lecturer of theology, wrote articles and offered private tuition on philosophy to wealthy Americans – including Isadora Duncan with whom he had an affair. While her husband was immersed in his work and his affair, Elsa became very isolated. During this time she was able to find her own way in life.

In many respects the United States offered the freedom that Elsa required to express herself. Many women in America were entering into the arts and the business world, feeling less restricted by European moral conventions and ideals. Technology and futurism were operating far in advance of sluggish European methods. And the lack of a real sense of history on the other side of the Atlantic brought with it an openness to modern thinking and experimentation. All of these things inspired Schiaparelli and gave her a different viewpoint on fashion and style to the wholly European-influenced Parisian designers with whom she was soon to become compared.

previous page The influence of Schiaparelli is seen clearly in the 1988 creation by Yves Saint Laurent

left Elsa Schiaparelli

above The 'Cravat' black and white woolen jumper with which Schiaparelli launched herself onto the Paris fashion scene

In 1920 Elsa became acquainted with Marcel Duchamp and Francis Picabia – two Parisians who had relocated in New York. Duchamp was a pioneer of the Dada-ist movement in painting, and Picabia a musician who imported the latest fashions from France. Duchamp and Picabia introduced Elsa to Baron de Meyer (the impressionist), Alfred Stieglitz (the artist-photographer), and, most importantly, the young Man Ray.

Although they all all understood and had experienced the European tradition they had the added perspective of life in the futuristic metropolis of New York. It was this group that subsequently introduced Elsa to a wider circle of artists when she moved to Paris in 1923. Among others she became friends with Jean Cocteau – with whom she would work on many designs later in life.

Once in Paris Elsa's career developed after she met the couturier Paul Poiret who encouraged her aspirations and almost adopted her as his successor in spirit. Poiret's designs were beyond the season with their almost costume like theatricality. Elsa made evening garments for many of her friends and Poiret's theatrical style was an influence in her designs.

In 1926 Elsa Schiaparelli formalised this dressmaking approach to fashion design and concentrated her efforts into Display No 1 – an exhibition of her first range of daywear held at her apartment. Consisting mainly of handknitted sweaters the range featured bold colours that acted as a contrast to the minimalist, sombre neutrals and monochrome colours that were fashionable at the time. The sweaters featured patterns inspired by modern technology; simplified down into Art Deco geometrics. Some featured grid structures – with echoes of Mondrian as well as Manhattan. Elsa was inspired by the newness going on around her and was keen to translate these cultural changes as pictures through clothing. Just as the traditional art world had been deconstructed through the modern movements of Impressionism, Dada-ism, Cubism and Surrealism, Elsa wanted to break down the barriers in pattern and print to feature more modern, relevant images. Geometrics and stripes reflected the machine aesthetic of the 20s but Elsa's *trompe l'oeil* designs more deeply fused art and fashion together .

After the success of Elsa's stunt at the Ritz Hotel lunch in 1927, *trompe l'oeil* in knitwear became a hallmark of her collections. She designed sweaters that featured knitted men's ties, handkerchiefs peaking out of pockets and crossword puzzles. Elsa developed the theme to include real details, so a *trompe l'oeile* belt would feature a genuine buckle and finally her *trompe l'oeile* masterpiece – a skeleton X-ray sweater.

Thus Elsa became known for novel, innovative print and pattern; always prompting a second glance, always a conversation piece and always identifiable as a Schiaparelli. In Display No 2 Elsa extended her range to incorporate sports and lounge wear including a bathing suit that featured a very low back and transparent straps giving the impression from behind that the wearer was nude. She also showed golden fish swimming across azure blue bodices for real underwater effect.

There then followed a career full of showstopping creations and collaborations that were to make Schiaparelli the most talked about and inspired designer of her time. Schiaparelli's major contribution to fashion

lay in her ability to override a trend and to create a unique masterpiece with timeless appeal – almost like a painting. Her ability to elevate clothing into a more intellectual expression drawing upon interesting references and influences was what attracted her to artists and visa versa. Many famous artists collaborated with Schiaparelli including Cocteau, Berard, Giacometti and Dali. Photographer Man Ray was a lifelong friend and companion as was Cecil Beaton.

left An advert in the unmistakable Schiaparelli style for her Shocking range of perfume, which actually coined the phrase 'shocking pink'

right A Cecil Beaton photograph of the 1936 Desk Suit by Schiaparelli, with bureau drawers for pockets, based on a drawing by Salvador Dali

above A punk T shirt based on designs by Jamie Reid featuring the Queen's portrait with safety pin and assorted graffiti/text

Many of the collaborations manifested themselves in the form of designer prints; one of the first being with Vertes who developed bold eclectic patterns featuring fairgrounds, animals, flying birds and insects as well as bold florals in modern Art Deco style. These prints were avidly copied for years and now represent the epitome in conversational prints which often feature in designer collections – notably at Chanel.

In 1938 Schiaparelli collaborated with Dali on a print that was not only revolutionary at the time but was also a great precursor of punk – the most Surrealist of statements in visual appearance. A long silk crepe column in ivory printed with *trompe l'oeil* tears and rips, was worn with a hood that featured real rips finished off to mirror the print of the dress. Post punk one is astonished at how modern the print looks. In 1938, to treat clothing with such daring vision and abstraction was unique and forward thinking. Punk's motifs of ripped fabric, montaged newspaper print and safety pin clasps were all features of Schiaparelli's collections in the 1930s. Schiaparelli's newspaper montage prints were inspired by a Picasso collage and aside from the headlines could have been designed in 1979. While the spirit of punk was not in any way connected with the work of Schiaparelli, she was certainly a punk in spirit in her desire to break down barriers in visual appearance and to shock – even calling her first fragrance Shocking. Another Dali collaboration from the same period featured a giant placement print of a lobster – a Surrealist motif that, among others, fascinated Schiaparelli in its mundanity.

above Schiaparelli's famous
'lobster' dress in white organdy with
a chiffon cummerbund, from 1937

left The 1938 precursor to punk,
the Dali-inspired silk crêpe tear dress
with a head scarf of actual torn fabric

Robe de Schiaparelli - 1937.

orné par Jean Cocteau.

Although well known for bold and daring prints, Elsa became even more renowned for her extravagant embroideries. She worked closely with Jean Cocteau on many designs developing the *trompe l'oeil* theme. On one jacket Cocteau sketched a Grecian urn filled with silk roses with the undulating curves of the urn composing two kissing faces. On another jacket Cocteau's design is signed and features golden bugle beaded hair flowing down one arm and an embroidered hand across the front of the jacket clutching a sequinned scarf.

Elsa's embroideries were extremely dramatic and went a long way to inspire many other couturiers including Yves St Laurent – who was a huge fan of Schiaparelli. Yves St Laurent, the master of embroidery since the 60s, worked closely with embroiderer Francois Lesage who in turn had worked with Schiaparelli. In 1980 Laurent featured a fitting tribute to Elsa in an all-

left A 1937 Schiaparelli creation with embroidered designs by Jean Cocteau including golden hair and a blue cellophane handerchief

right Moschino's take on fashion and surrealism, from 1988

over embroidery called *Les Yeux d'Elsa*. He also paid homage to many great artists via fantastical embroideries; Braque's doves held together the fluid silk of a toga dress at a single point on the shoulder, Dali's lips were depicted on a sequinned coat, and the work of Cocteau in a rococo mirror motif jacket.

Yves St Laurent like Schiaparelli, has been genuinely influenced by artists throughout his life. His Mondrian dress of the early 60s was true living art and perfectly summed up the modern attitude of the time, even though it was influenced by a piece of art from 40 years earlier. Similarly, his pop art silhouette dress inspired by Magritte shows his understanding of fashion as more than just clothing.

As well as creating Surrealist images through print and embroidery Schiaparelli's ranges featured witticisms in 3D. Novelty buttons were a major statement in many collections; butterflies, bugs, acrobats and dancing horses all added a Surreal twist to a garment. And in 1936 Schiaparelli developed her desk suit, based on a drawing by Dali. The suit featured a series of true and false pockets that looked like drawers, with buttons for knobs. It was a major influence on the work of 80s designer Franco Moschino. Moschino's collections were a sea of surrealist witticisms, in 3D and in print, that transcended seasonal trends. Many reference points were taken directly from Schiaparelli with the black and white *trompe l'oeil* of Elsa's early work being re-interpreted in many guises. Elsa's desk suit concept was recreated with 3D coin purses and envelopes for pockets and images of lips, fish and hearts recurring throughout. While Yves St Laurent continued to emulate Elsa'a beautifully executed Surreal embroideries, Moschino was her successor in translating Surreal witticism through fashion.

Schiaparelli's links with Surrealism extended beyond her collections and into her advertising and promotional campaigns. Working with Man Ray and Cecil Beaton, she helped to create some of the most innovative fashion plates of the 20th Century. For the launch of her fragrance Shocking in 1938 Schiaparelli used the figure of actress Mae West as the basis for an hourglass figure flacon that depicted surrealist style in an illustrative poster campaign.

Fashion and Surrealism have enjoyed a love affair ever since Schiaparelli cemented the bond. Yves St Laurent and Moschino have certainly been the designers most heavily influenced by her, but others have also brought Surrealist imagery into their clothing. Designers with an inherent sense of humour in fashion often relate to the fusion. Paul Smith has often featured photographic repeat prints of fruit, fish and newspaper montages. Vivienne Westwood plays with artist's representation of the body on the top of the body and her padded skirts reflect the distortion of the body seen in Surrealist photography and sculpture. Karl Lagerfeld nods a gesture of respect to Sciaparelli via conversational prints at Chanel, and Philip Treacy the milliner works with designers such as John Galliano in creating Surrealist fantasies for the head.

As fashion becomes more and more retrospective and repetitive in its references, Surrealism as an influence continues to interest and inspire – with the spirit of the unexpected still remaining.

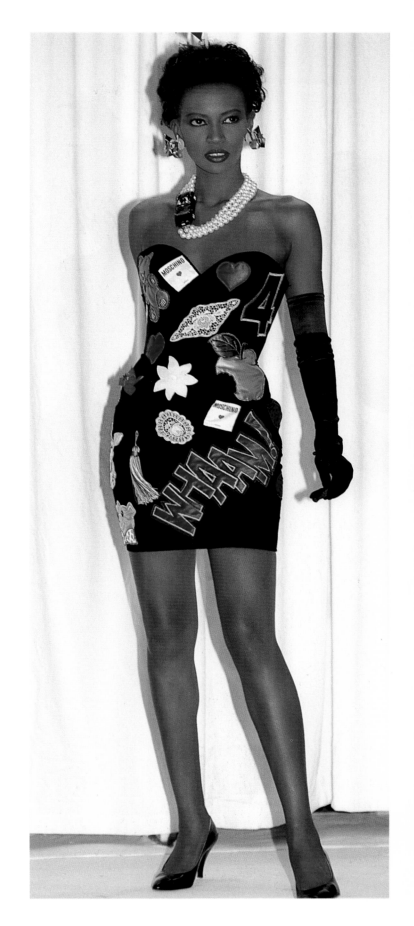

8

dior's new look

The most significant moment in post-war fashion occurred on 12 February 1947. There was a coal shortage in France and Paris shivered in temperatures of 13 degrees below freezing. Most of the American fashion buyers had already left the city. Lelong, Balmain, Rochas, Piguet, Fath and Balenciaga had already shown their spring-summer ranges. But a newcomer, Christian Dior, had still to show his debut collection.

When Carmel Snow, editor of *Harper's Bazaar* sat down in Dior's new salon on the Avenue Montaigne, she hissed: 'This had better be good.'

This hiss was followed by another – the unfamiliar swish of huge petticoats as they swung from the wasp-waist of Dior's models. Ernestine Carter of British *Harper's Bazaar* captured the moment: 'Arrogantly swinging their vast skirts, the soft shoulders, the tight bodices, the wasp-waists, the tiny hats bound on by veils under the chin, they swirled on, contemptuously bowling over the ashtray stands like ninepins. This new softness and soundness was positively voluptuous.'

Some of the audience cheered; others wept. Another eyewitness, Janet Ironside, who went on to become professor of fashion design at London's Royal College of Art, was enraptured.

'It was like a new love affair' she said, 'the first sight of Venice, a new chance, in fact a new look at life.'

What was so revolutionary about Dior's collection was that for eight years fashion had been frozen. During World War II, wartime regulations had stipulated that nothing should go out of style before it wore out. The length of skirts, the amount of fabric used, even the number of pockets, pleats and buttonholes were strictly controlled and any sort of unnecessary padding or decoration was outlawed.

But Dior flew in the face of all that. It took up to 25 yards of material to make a Dior skirt. The regulations stipulated three. Because of the war, for years, clothes had been simple and practical. Dior's were wild and extravagant. He constricted his models in corsets. Their hips and bras were padded. Padded shoulders – the only piece of shaping that had survived the war – were skewed, making shoulders round rather than square.

Dior called his collection 'Corolla' – like the whorl of a leaf or a flower before it blossoms. His 'Figure of Eight' line took this shape even further, with the waist narrowed and the hips and breasts moulded and accentuated. Carmel Snow remarked that the New York buyers who had fled the cold of Paris before Dior's show had better come back.

'It's quite a revolution, dear Christian,' she told Dior after the show. 'Your dresses have such a new look.'

previous page Dior's dramatic 'Envol' or 'Flight' line of 1948, which had the skirt caught up at the back and stiffened to jut out over its underskirt

above The master Christian Dior, at the height of his fame in 1950

right Dior seamstresses making up a 45cm. waist skirt which uses over 45 meters of material!

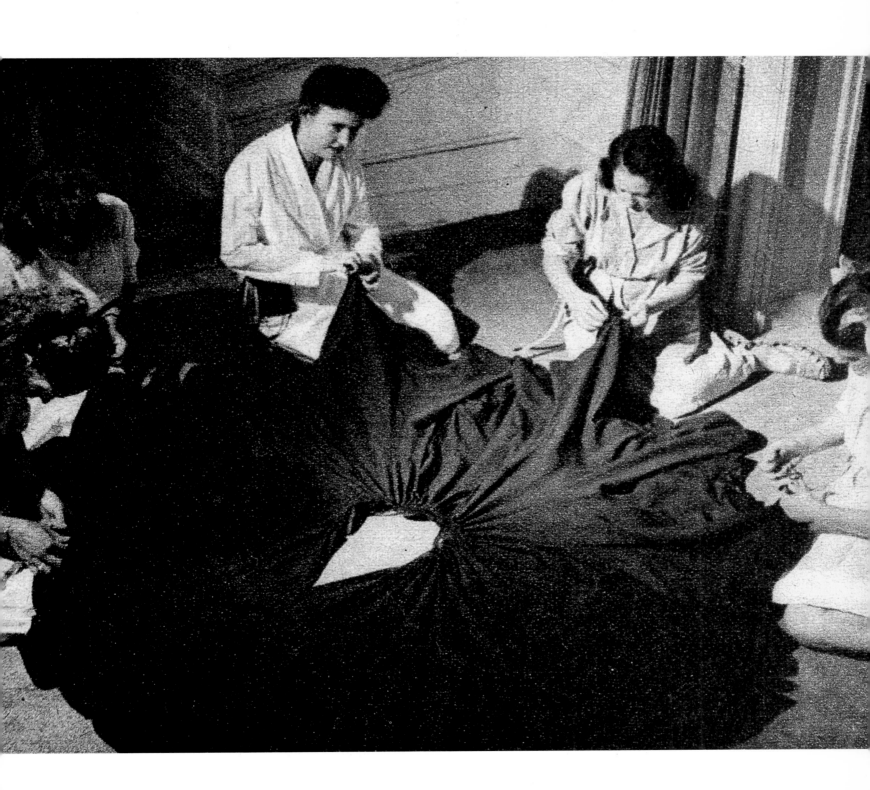

In 1947, Dior was an unknown. The news wires even mis-spelt his name as Diaure or d'Yorre. But *Life* magazine picked up on the two words 'New Look' and they stuck. Soon even the French were calling Monsieur Dior's new line 'Le New Look'.

However, the New Look was not universally welcomed. In Paris, women demonstrated at its blatant extravagance, complaining that Dior was charging 40,000 francs for a dress when French children had no milk to drink. At that time, a school teacher earned 9,000 francs a month and oil, milk and dairy products were still rationed.

In March 1947, Dior tried to stage a fashion shoot in the markets of Montemartre, but women in the market were so outraged that they tore the clothes off the models' backs. Women who walked in the street wearing New Look fashion were abused by passers-by. But women who could afford Dior's creations were in the fitting rooms after the show buying his dresses as soon as the models took them off.

The American government thought the New Look was a scandal. How could a Frenchman be so unpatriotic to squander huge amounts of material when his country was nearly bankrupt? The answer was that Dior's newly created couture house was backed by Marcel Boussac, a textile magnate. If hemlines plummeted and pleats were piled on more pleats, he would turn a tidy profit.

The US authorities considered censorship to prevent news of the New Look getting back to America. But the war was over and the press would brook no more restrictions. It was hard to be see how a new line of couture fashions could be a threat to national security.

Many American women had enjoyed the freedom wartime casual clothes had given them and did not want to return to restricting corsets. They picketed stores where the New Look was sold and, when Dior himself turned up in New York in September 1947, they marched down the street shouting: 'Burning Christian Dior.'

'You and your so-called genius have succeeded in disfiguring my wife,' wrote a farmer in Idaho, and an engineer from Texas warned: 'Set foot in this state and I will kick you out.'

Unperturbed, Dior headed for Dallas where he received the Neiman-Marcus award for his contribution. Needless to say, the engineer did not make good on his threat.

One woman founded the 'A Little Below the Knee' Club in protest. Soon it had 1,300 members in 48 states. The San Antonio chapter pledged: 'The Alamo fell, but our hemlines will not.' They were wrong.

The Georgia state legislature tried to outlaw the New Look. Cartoonists in every paper in the country tried to ridicule it out of existence. They failed. Dior was sanguine in the face of his critics. Those women who protest the most will wearing the longest skirts, he said.

In Britain, the President of the Board of Trade, Sir Stafford Cripps (who at the time was preocupied with the rigours of rationing) complained that the it was 'utterly stupid and irresponsible that time, labour, materials and money should be wasted on these imbecilities'.

A Liverpool Member of Parliament, Bessie Braddock, condemned the New Look as 'the ridiculous whim of idle people'.

right A foundation garment from Dior's 1947 New Look, described by *Vogue* as 'a taffeta underbodice with rose ruffles at the breasts'

left Wartime chic: a Cecil Beaton photograph from the pages of British *Vogue* in 1942

right An illustration featuring a New Look dress set in Maxim's restaurant, Paris, from *Vogue*, 1947

Left-winger Mabel Ridealgh MP saw it as a more pernicious threat.

'Ridiculous, stupidly exaggerated waste of material and manpower, foisted on the average woman to the detriment of normal clothing,' she said. 'Our modern world has become used to the freedom of short, sensible clothing. The New Look is reminiscent of a caged bird's attitude. I hope our fashion dictators will realise the new outlook of women and give the death blow to any attempt to curtail women's freedom.'

But women had been starved of fashion throughout the war. Styles had remained drab and static. Now the war was over they wanted clothes that were brash, fun and extravagant; clothes that expressed a new optimism.

Men returning from the front were sick of seeing women in uniforms. They wanted their wives and sweethearts to be rounded and feminine again. Dior himself pointed out that there was nothing new about the New Look. He had copied the clothes he had seen his mother wearing during the Belle Époque, the period of peace and stability before the Great War.

It was Dior, rather than the politicians and backwoodsmen, who had judged the mood of the time correctly. The movie stars were the first to come around, after Rita Hayworth wore a Dior gown called 'Soirée' to the premiere of her film Gilda. The rich and famous found New Look fashions were a way to flaunt their wealth. It was hardly practical to wear the New Look to work in an office or a shop. One Dior coat had no sleeves and could only be put on or taken off with the help of a maid.

In Britain, the economy was in ruins and, although the war was over, rationing became more severe under the Labour government's new 'austerity programme'. The fabric for just one New Look skirt would use up more than an entire year's clothing coupons. However, with ingenuity, it was possible to get around the regulations. The dressmakers Dereta made 700 New Look suits in unrationed grey flannel, and sold out in two weeks.

The big department stores began selling slimmed down version of Dior's designs, while ordinary women found a use for the blackout curtains they had taken down when the air raids were over.

Butterick Paper Patterns came up with a number of novel ways to give a New Look styling to old fashioned, knee-length skirts. One way was to unpick an old dirndl skirt and turn the fabric lengthways to give it extra length. Women would also combine two old garments to make one New Look skirt.

In the Palace, the two princesses, Elizabeth and Margaret Rose, naturally wanted to keep up with the latest fashions. This caused a problem. The royal family could hardly be seen to be flouting government regulations. The couturier Molyneux came to the rescue. He sewed broad velvet bands around the bottom of Princess Margaret's coat, widening the skirt and lengthening the hem.

On the Continent, shortages were even more severe. Young Dutch girls produced New Look dresses out made of patchwork, sewed together with thread they had made by unravelling old fabric. As a patriotic flourish, they would add a strip of orange – the national colour – around the hem. And to make a tight-fitting New Look-style top, they would use US Army-issue T-shirts, heralding the style of the 1950s and 1960s.

By spring 1948, all the Paris couture houses were showing New Look designs. Skirts were full; waists nipped; shoulders dropped. Bodices were structured; bosoms full; hips and derrières were padded.

In London, Molyneux launched a British version of the New Look, which was instantly dubbed the London Look. Princess Margaret wore a London Look dress on her visit to Paris in May 1948. According to Nancy Mitford, Dior, who had already dropped his mid-calf hemlines to the ankle, hated it. But he realised that, although he had begun the New Look, it was not longer his alone. By autumn, he had raised his hemlines again to 14 inches from the ground.

Princess Margaret was converted to Dior though. For her 21st birthday party, she ordered a ballgown from his 'Lily-of-the-Valley' collection. It had a full, floor-length skirt made in white silk organza, with a front panel embroidered with flowers and foliage in straw tone, spangles and mother of pearl. The bodice was padded. A broad shoulder strap covered one shoulder – the other was left bare. The New Look now had royal approval.

Over the next ten years following 1947, Dior came up with numerous variations on the New Look, season by season. Although he drew inspiration from the 'Directoire' and 'Empire' periods, his designs became more wearable and practical for ordinary women. He no longer needed controversy. He only needed to be known for style.

The controversy around the launch of the New Look had done its work. It had made the Dior name recognisable around the world. He was as famous as Gandhi or Stalin. Dior had started in 1947 with three workshops and a staff of 85. Soon he had 28 workshops and 1,400 staff. Twenty-five thousand customers trooped through his salon each season, with 60 per cent of its sales going to the US.

Although Dior was the new kid on the block, the rest of the Parisian couture houses were not jealous of his success. For five years they had been cut off from their markets in Britain and America behind German lines. Now Dior had single-handedly made Paris the capital of haute couture again. Fashion was such a lucrative export industry that a grateful French government awarded Dior the Légion d'Honneur in 1950.

Maison Dior also became the prototype of the modern fashion house. Until Dior came along, couturiers would look down their noses at ready-to-wear lines. Dior had no qualms about putting his name on mass produced garments. He also sold stockings, brassieres, girdles, handbags, gloves, shoes, ties, swim-suits and jewellery. These were made in 87 countries. He set up branches in London, New York and Caracas. Companies in Canada, Australia, Santiago and Cuba took reproduction contracts. He turned haute couture from a cottage industry into a huge international business.

And it was Dior who came up with the most profitably item sold by any couture house, the fragrance. As a tribute to his sister, Dior launched the perfume Miss Dior – the English name was used deliberately to court the American market.

Dior's later lines - the A, H, Y, Windmill and Eiffel Tower - were widely copied too. But it was the New Look that marked a sea change. Artists, architects and designers of glass, furniture, wallpaper, crockery and other household goods all drew inspiration from Dior and his influence could be seen far beyond the bounds of fashion.

When Coco Chanel returned to the world of couture fashion in 1954, she became one of Dior's sternest critics.

'Balenciaga?' she said. 'He dresses women to look like old Spaniards. Dior? To look like armchairs. He puts covers on them.'

There was some truth to this. Dior covered and shaped women's bodies, rather than revealing their natural shape as Chanel did. But Dior was amused by Chanel's comments rather than hurt. She had her place in the history of fashion, but was now a spent force.

'Chanel had created fashion for elegant women rather than for those that are pretty,' Dior said.

FROM THE NEW LOOK

Below : Last season's hat was a wide shovel, last season's jacket was loose and finger-tip length. This season's hat is a cone, this season's jacket is a mere bolero matching your dress.

THE NEW LOOK   THE NOW LOOK

THE NEW LOOK   THE NOW LOOK

Above : Last season's accessories were a biggish handbag and an umbrella. This season's accessory is a stole, of fur or fabric bordered with fur, wrapped round you with luxurious warmth.

Right : Last season's dress was strapless and bare. This season's dress is strapless, too, but you shroud your shoulders in a scarf or a shawl of embroidered chiffon or cobwebby lace.

40

THE NEW LOOK   THE NOW LOOK

The thrust of Chanel's argument what that Dior's clothes were sexist. Dior's women were expected to stand around in the cold with their shoulders and half their busts exposed, delightful ornaments for the consumption of men. To be fair, Dior made clothes for movie stars, royalty and the super-rich, who were assertive enough to look after themselves. If other women followed Dior's fashions, that was their choice.

left A 1951 portrait of Princess Margaret by Cecil Beaton wearing the 21st birthday dress by Dior

right A spread celebrating the continuing appeal of the New Look from *Harpers Bazaar*, November 1948

right Alice Dodd models John Galliano in his first collection when he moved to Dior in 1997

In the 1950s, Dior was the king of haute couture, the master technician. He could change fashion at a whim, or so he thought. When he tried to take some of Chanel's criticisms on board, he found himself slated in the press for abandoning the structured style of the New Look. Dior arrogantly dismissed these attacks.

'Better to be slated in three columns on the front page than congratulated in two lines on the inside,' he said.

The other fashion houses were in a quandary, but they were obliged to follow where Dior led. This sudden reversal was too much for the customers to follow though, so in 1955 Dior turned back with his A line. One design he came up was the 'Adele', a style that became de rigueur for young girls in the late 1950s. The skirt was flared over net petticoats and reached just below the knee. The top was a short-sleeved, shirt-waister, tightly clinched into a small waist in its natural position.

Christian Dior died on 24 October 1957. He was 52. He was succeeded at Maison Dior by the 21-year-old Yves Saint Laurent, who Dior had taken under his wing when he was 17. At first, Saint Laurent developed Dior's lines, and was seen as a worthy successor. But in 1960 the world was changing, and in response Saint Laurent launched his 'Beat Look', which drew its inspiration from the leather-jacketed bikers and 'existentialist' students of the Left Bank quarter of Paris. However, the chic Parisian women of the Right Bank did not want to wear black leather. So Yves Saint Laurent had to go.

He was succeeded by Marc Bohan who had worked at Piguet's, Molyneux's and Patou's before heading Maison Dior in London. Bohan reverted to Dior's lines. Yves Saint Laurent went on to found a hugely successful couture house of his own.

In the 1970s, Maison Dior branched out into menswear. A series of take-overs did little to improve its fortunes until, in 1997, it brought in the flamboyant British designer John Galliano in a bid to put the House of Dior back in the forefront of the fashion world, as it had been when Christian Dior introduced the New Look 50 years before.

Although Galliano's first collection for Maison Dior created a great deal of interest, it could not compete with the launch of the New Look. No fashion before or since has been greeted with riots in the streets, the threat of censorship, the censure of governments and a mass protest movement.

Dior summed up the appeal of the New Look succinctly.

'I brought back the art of pleasing,' he said.

above Model Eva Herzigova in the John Galliano debut collection for the House of Dior in 1997

marlon
brando –
streetcool
streetwise

When Marlon Brando and Lee Marvin rode into the American consciousness in 1953 a rebellion was born. The film was *The Wild One*, and starred a youthful Brando playing the part of Johnny a mixed up angry young man, who became a symbol of teenage rebellion in the 50s.

The film is set in a small town in California, Brando is part of a gang of bikers hell bent on destroying the peace. In black leather biker jackets, T shirts and battered jeans, they cruise into town on their shining Triumph motorbikes, all bad attitude and looking for trouble. The film caused a stir - it was even banned in Britain until the late 60s - and the biker uniform became the symbol of youthful rebellion influencing American teenagers through the 50s and beyond. Such a film would seem inocuous now, but this was 1953 and post-war America was a conservative place.

With the ravages and uncertainties of the Second World War still foremost in the collective American mind, the safe and normal was everyone's dream. Family values were paramount and traditional had became the American way. Life couldn't be better. In America, and later Europe there was full employment. What we take for granted now as modern life was just beginning. The consumer society was getting underway with cheap goods available to everyone and nine out of ten US households already owned a television set.

Behind the suburban picket garden fences and bourgeois niceties, social insecurity was gaining ground. The world was changing. The cold war had just begun and the atom bomb had become a reality. Now that television could beam out visual images of world affairs, the young were able to see exactly what was going on. This heady cocktail of material affluence in a world where the old values were changing so rapidly had its impact very strongly on the young. Against the backdrop of a dubious future, their parents complacency seemed at odds with the troubles around, and the young started to ask questions.

The young had begun to find a voice of their own, and once the teenage movement had been set in motion, it gathered pace until it exploded in the turbulent 60s and has continued gaining power ever since. The emergence of this new social class was only made possible by the unique set of factors which characterised the early 50s. Full employment meant the young had their pick of jobs, and with money in their pockets to buy the new street styles, they became a marketing dream. As their spending power grew, the marketing people and advertisers were quick to exploit this new market force and cheap mass produced clothes became available exclusively for the young.

They started to wear fashions that suited their mood instead of that which suited their parents. This seems hardly remarkable now, but in those days the powerful 'youth culture' simply didn't exist. Children were children until suddenly catapulted into adulthood. Young people looked like miniature versions of their parents, well dressed and respectable.

right and previous page Marlon Brando as Johnny in *The Wild One*, the role that was to create the classic biker image for all time

BE REALLY REFRESHED... GRADUATE TO COKE

Upperclass refreshment... Coke! Only Coca-Cola gives you the cheerful lift that's bright and lively... the col
crisp taste that deeply satisfies... the pause that refreshes... anytime... anywhere! Pause often... for Coke

Get Coke in King Size, too.
Now available almost everywhere.

 **Enjoy Coca-Cola** for THE PAUSE THAT REFRESHE

King · Regular

As the 50s progressed, kids broke away from the parental stronghold and started doing their own thing. Dressed in their own style and with economic independence from their parents, these new affluent young consumers became a class in themselves. With their new found wealth they were quick to spend their money on the new young clothes. The American college look which had gained popularity as the 50s introduced a more casual approach to dress. With the leisure age gaining ground, drip dry fabrics had become available and more colourful casual clothes were being worn. In their clean cut Ivy League clothes he was a feature at high school campuses drinking soda pops at the local drive in. A somewhat more colourful version of his father, he would wear a loosely fitting sports shirt with maybe Hawaiian print or some other colourful design. In keeping with the idea of leisure was the cardigan and sports jacket worn with chinos or slacks and penny loafers.

Young girls dressed in the style of the girl next door screen idols, typified by Doris Day and Debbie Reynolds. Squeaky clean in their full length skirts over layers of petticoats bobby socks and penny loafers this was not the sexually inviting look of the sex siren. They would sometimes wear trousers with a side zip; a front zip was thought to provocative. Like the boys, young girls got on the denim trend and wore them with turn ups and patterned blouses, with their hair tied back in a ponytail. Young and hedonistic, they wanted immediate pleasure and constant change.

left Brigitte Bardot proved that a ponytail, T shirt and blue jeans could be sexy rather than squeaky clean

far left The American college look; colourful and casual without a hint of teen trauma or rock'n'roll rebellion

dangerous combination of black leather and rough and ready jeans was not. The image of the delinquent was born and perceived hooliganism was on the way up. In today's society where provocation is almost *de rigeur*, Johnny's outfit and behaviour seems mild, but in the 1950s it was a disturbing departure from the norm that was laden with violent overtones and sexual undertones.

But why had Johnny chosen the prosaic clothes of the workman? For the first time, nonconformity was shown by dressing down. Rebelling against prosperous society in the 1950s meant going a step down the socio-economic ladder, and wearing working class clothes to give authenticity to what they were trying to say. Young people didn't want to identify with the straight laced, responsible attitudes of their fathers, and so dressed like a youthful version of the working man. Society was smart, squeaky clean and aspirational, Brando and his followers were scruffy, downbeat and unkempt.

Until the 50s most street looks had taken their inspiration from the upper classes. Even the velvet collared draped jackets and 'drainpipe' trousers of the 1950s British Teddy Boys (the London version of the teenage hoodlum) gentleman's clothes of the Edwardian era (hence the 'Teddy'), but when the 1950s American teenager put on his T shirt and jeans, he was borrowing directly from the attire of the manual labourer.

The T shirt was adapted from the working man's vest or under shirt, and with its short casual sleeves it exposed the muscles of the arm denoting physical work. The black leather jacket, designed by the Schott brothers in New York was an adaptation of the Second World War fighter jacket and carried with it all its heroic connotations. Biker boots, strong and sturdy, were clearly not meant to be worn in the office or down the local diner. But when the teenager put on his blue jeans the look was perfect.

The 50s heralded the beginning of jeans as day wear. Invented by Levi Strauss during the 1849 gold rush, they were traditionally worn by miners, farmers and cowboys, pillars of the American way of life. But ironically, the association with manual labour also came to represent a rejection of middle class values. They became a powerful unisex item and were worn by teenagers across the board. Indeed, by the late 60s they had become almost a badge of rebellion against mainstream society worldwide.

Taken as a whole, the look is a romantic appropriation of real practical clothes and when they are put together, they carry with them all the image of toil and harsh working conditions. Variations on the biker look were worn, and boys could be seen hanging around in denim jackets or bum freezer jackets, plaid shirts and of course the ubiquitous jeans.

Not that the 1950s teenager had any intention to go and work in the fields, being more content to 'hang loose' on street corners or down the local pool hall, but it was the embodiment of these values which was important. By wearing this classless uniform they disassociated themselves from their comfortable family life and all its attendant restraints. It was rough and reeked of rejection of family values. Even if you had a place secured at university and your parents lived in the suburbs, when the leather jacket was on, you were suddenly a 'punk' from the wrong side of the tracks.

When Rock'n'Roll burst onto the scene in the mid 50s the kids were absolutely ready for it. Youth power had begun, and when the film *Blackboard Jungle* appeared in 1954 showing delinquent teenagers terrorising a school (to the accompaniment of Bill Haley's 'Rock Around The Clock') the Establishment was shocked. But the teenage ball was rolling, and there was no stopping it.

And along with rock and roll and new found freedom, juvenile delinquency became almost a fashion in itself, as much with those who made it their business to condemn it as with the minority of teenagers who actually practised it.

Not everyone wanted to toe the line, which brings us back to Johnny. When Johnny and the rest of the bad boys walked into that Californian town their message was clear. This was sartorial provocation at its loudest, and a warning signal to 'straight' society. By defying the stylistic mores of their elders and wearing an outfit so out of keeping with the status quo they were openly challenging the American way and all that went with it. Bobby socks and college loafers were different but acceptable, the

SOME GALS WILL DO **ANYTHING** FOR **KICKS!**

ROCK 'N ROLL GAL

By ERNIE WEATHERALL

35¢
B 131

THE SIZZLING WORLD OF REAL GONE GUYS—AND DOLLS ON DOPE!

left The white vest or T shirt hunk/punk was another archetype created by Brando in *A Streetcar Named Desire*, and aped in movies and pulp fiction throughout the 50s

Hollywood soon caught on to this new audience with money to spend on Saturday night at the pictures, and were quick to cash in on the emerging subcultural style. When the film *Rebel Without A Cause* was released, it gave teenage angst and delinquency a whole new kind of street credibility. James Dean as Jim, unable to communicate with his fussy, straight laced parents, influenced a whole generation of teenagers with his moody good looks and sullen performance. But it was the appeal of the local gang in the film, with their unkempt jeans-and-sneakers style and flick knives which romanticised the hoodlum. If you hadn't bought your Perfecto and put on your air of defiance after watching this film you were clearly on the side of the 'squares'.

These teenage cults were stylised in the late 50s hit musical *West Side Story*. Two rival gangs of Puerto Ricans and the Americans spent their time getting out their flick knives and organising 'rumbles' dressed in their turn up jeans, T shirts and wind breaker jackets.

The American 'punk' look clearly distinguished the cool cats from the 'squares' and had become an American social phenomenon. But although the 1950s delinquent gave way to the piece loving hippie in the 1960s, the classic biker look has never gone away. Taking on a far wider appeal than the original 50s hoodlum, the biker look has been used time and time again as the symbol of subversion and anti establishment since Johnny stepped into that cafe back in 1953.

left Russ Tamblyn as Riff, leader of the Jets gang in the movie version of the Leonard Bernstein/Stephen Sondheim musical *West Side Story*

But whereas Johnny's gang of bikers only hinted at violence, as society became less naive and more violent, the biker image took on more brutal and extreme characteristics. In the 1960s a new set of bikers emerged. The Greasers – in Britain, the Rockers – were bad boys on bikes who terrorised towns and relished in their hell-breaking reputation. They wore their jeans filthy and soaked in oil, their hair was lank and dirty, they wore military helmets or peaked leather caps, and their prized leather jackets were covered in badges, insignia and chains. Sometimes they would wear cut-down denim jackets so soiled they were grey instead of blue.

If the 50s punks wanted to be bad then the Greasers had clearly seemed to have made a pact with some darker force. Their purposeful down-dressing and deliberate dirtiness was a sartorial indication that they were completely at odds with straight society and rejected all its values. They relished their reputation as terrifying outlaws, personified most famously in the Hell Angels who originated in Southern California but soon spawned imitators worldwide.

left Member of the Johannesburg, South Africa, Hell's Angels; the US cult could be found worldwide

The biker look was adopted once again when the punks hit the music and fashion scene in the late 1970s. Worn with metal studs and bondage trousers, the black leather jacket with its connotations of danger and rebellion was the perfect garment to epitomise their aggressive anarchy and nihilistic 'no hope' attitude.

Finally by the 80s, the rebellious uniform of T shirt, jeans and leather jacket had been absorbed into the mainstream and become normal everyday wear. Although jeans were now worn by the middle aged as well as the young, the black leather jacket still carried with it a certain rebellious cachet. It became the uniform for many rock musicians from Lou Reed to Sheryl Crow. Guitar in hand and sod-you snarl, the jacket gave the finishing touches to their usually affected look of defiance.

If the rock musician has taken the jacket to show their freedom from the 'normal' then the early 80s homosexual took the look and made it into a lifestyle. From the rock band Village People to the streets of the Castro district in San Francisco, moustached bikers with leather jackets, white T shirts and tight denim jeans, walk arm in arm in defiance of 'straight' society. With its anti establishment symbolism, it fits in very well with the gay idea of remaining outside the heterosexual lifestyle norm of the family unit. James Dean and Marlon Brando with their macho yet pretty good looks and image of the sullen loner have always been gay icons.

This look with its raw sexuality and rebellious connotations was too good to rest on the fringes of society, and by the early 1990s, as retro fashion was gaining popularity, an authentic version of the biker uniform was worn by working and middle class boys eager to look like an extra in *West Side Story* or *Rebel Without A Cause*. The romantic connotation of the 50s was recreated, although the rebellion was lost, out of context of its original time and social situation.

In the late 80s the black leather jacket was finally appropriated by mainstream fashion designers who modified and watered down any rebellious significance, in order to send it out onto the catwalk as an innocuous fashion garment. Designers like Katherine Hamnett, Jean Paul Gaultier, Sonia Rykel and Gianni Versace have all presented glammed-up versions of the Perfecto jacket.

It is interesting that a street style which started off on the backs of the 50s teenager as a sign of youthful rebellion designed to shock the world of their parents is now the most sought after commodity in the fashion industry. Top 'street' designers like Dolce & Gabbana and Prada, hungry for the next look on the street, regularly trawl nightclubs and bars, only to rediscover the black leather jacket, tart it up and send it down the catwalk in an even more anodyne, high fashion version.

right The leather jacket as haute couture, in 90s fashion collections from Valentino (top) and Versace

10 mary quant and the miniskirt

10

One of the most enduring images of the 1960s is undoubtedly the miniskirt. Not merely a new fashion trend, but a true icon of the 60s, the miniskirt epitomised the attitudes of the era . The name synonymous with the fame of the miniskirt was of course Mary Quant. Not only was she responsible for creating the infamous miniskirt, but she also led the way for radical changes in the fashion industry which made London such a celebrated centre of cultural importance during the 1960s. Like most new fashion trends, the miniskirt was an innovative idea sparked off by a series of unique social and cultural changes. Hemlines had been dramatically shortened before the 1960s , also during times of great social change.

After WW1, advances in female emancipation, along with post war escapism and the exciting innovative new fashions being shown by designers like Poiret and Chanel all contributed to an inevitable revolution in fashion. During the mid 20s, the prevailing fashion was androgynous, with women wearing short loose-fitting tubular dresses, bobbed hair styles and 'boyish' flattened chests. The women wearing this look were referred to as 'flappers' who seemed to enjoy a hedonistic celebration of the new era with no looking back. At the end of the previous century, the only part of a woman's body that had been visible from beneath her dress were her toes. By 1927 it was her leg up to the knee!

Three years later hemlines dropped considerably to a more sober calf length as part of a return to a more nostalgically romantic style. The end of the 30s saw hemlines shorten once more but not as drastically as the 20s. This time hemlines only went up as far as just below the knee, mainly due to mandatory fabric rationing during WW2.

After the Second World War, hemlines dropped again with Dior's extravagant, compared to austerity clothes, use of fabric in the New Look collection of 1947. The New Look , was mature and sophisticated, giving an exaggerated nipped-in hourglass shape to women, which was not appropriate for young women of the newly emerging post war generation. Previously young women had been expected to dress in the style of their mothers, which was usually loosely based on Parisian couture. These young women were now being exposed to totally new ideas in fashion, with a spirit inspired by the current cultural and social changes.

In America teenagers had already come into their own, forcing their elders to finally recognise adolescence as being different than childhood. Youths wore a new style of casual clothes designed for everyday wear, including denim work jeans. This trend coincided with the advent of mass publicity on Hollywood stars, who were photographed in exotic locations around the world wearing the latest in American leisurewear.

By the early 50s, American youth culture began to inspire British teenagers. This post war era saw the dawn of art colleges and fashion schools which became places to rebel, to be unique and to express yourself. Entrepreneurial thinking and originality were encouraged in these new institutions.

previous page Mary Quant at work, looking like the archetypal 60s 'dolly bird' that she helped create

right Granny Takes a Trip, one of the Kings Road boutiques in the 1960s that sprung up in the wake of Mary Quant's Bazaar

GRANNY TAKES A TRIP

SHOP &
BASEMENT
OPEN
10- 7

This generation was too young to remember the war clearly, and they were growing up rebellious and articulate, full of their own opinions and scornful of their parent's handling of world affairs amid the increased threat of nuclear war shadowed by the increasing number of atomic bomb testings. The British tested their first atomic bomb in 1952, the same year that the Americans had tested the first hydrogen bomb. Some women voiced their disapproval publicly in an anti-fashion, anti-establishment dress code. These young women moved away from the Paris fashions, which they considered bourgeois, towards a style which was much more their own. Black stockings, short hip-hugging skirts and pinafore dresses, and baggy sweaters worn over tight trousers were a few of the new looks, influenced by the beatnik movement in America and the existentialists of the Parisian Left Bank.

right What made 'Swinging London' swing – two models in classic 1965 'op art' dresses in Carnaby Street

Another social change which was affecting the direction of fashion was the new wealth of youth. Full employment, expanding trade and the introduction of extended payment purchases or 'HP' gave young people a new kind of prosperity, especially amongst the working class. This new spending power greatly influenced the fashion industry, as young people could now determine the direction of fashion since they wanted clothes that expressed their own attitudes and tastes, not those of their parent's.

In response to this new generation of consumers, French couture houses moved away from the sculpted wasp waisted look to a much simpler line. In 1954 Dior launched the H-line followed by the A-line in 1957. A young designer at the house of Dior named Yves Saint Laurent took the A-line even further, creating the 'trapeze' dress, which had a slightly shorter hemline. In the same year the unfitted 'sack' dress was launched, which had a tapered skirt which fell just below the knee. The following year saw the formation of the Campaign for Nuclear Disarmament.

By this time a young British designer named Mary Quant had already captured the mood of the moment. She represented a distinctive breakaway in fashion, evolving out of the ideas of the day's youth, having nothing to do with the established Paris fashion houses. Mary Quant opened her first shop, Bazaar, on the King's Road in London, with her partner and future husband, Alexander Plunket Greene in 1955.

Quant's early designs were inspired by the looks being worn by female students; an early indication of how ideas could come from 'the street' as easily as from the couturiers sketches. The early Quant dresses, which fell just below the knee, were neat little pinafores and sleeveless dresses worn over a blouse. They were simple yet unconventional when compared to Paris designs. They were also very affordable to the rapidly growing market of teenage girls, which was of utmost importance. The image was young and classless, and far removed from the fashions of teenage girl's mothers.

The fashion revolution coincided with the other big cultural change of the century: pop music. In 1954 Bill Haley performed 'Rock Around the Clock' to a riotous crowd, demonstrating the powerful influence that this new 'popular music' had on the young generation. By 1960 a teenager's main expenditure was on records and clothes. 'Melody bars' and record shops became a key place for teenagers to meet, 'hang out' and exchange ideas on fashion and music. Another popular meeting place was the Italian cafes, which had sprung up all over London following the mass immigration of Italians after the war. This new trend encouraged an element of Italian styling to creep into fashion, particularly in sportswear and casual separates.

In 1961 Quant opened her second Bazaar boutique in fashionable Knightsbridge, London, the same year that the new contraceptive pill became available. Hundreds of similar boutiques were to open in London, following the huge success of Bazaar. Now designers like Mary Quant were turning London into the new fashion capital, stealing the crown away from Paris. This was further confirmed by the success of Mary Quant's wholesale operation, founded in 1963, called The Ginger Group. Quant achieved her international recognition through the wholesale division which offered an affordable off-the-peg designer collection. Young women could now afford to buy a new different style every week. Easy-care,washable fabrics were more attractive than Paris couture quality to the average teenage girl with a hectic lifestyle. It was the inventiveness of British fashion designers combined with their mass produced off-the- peg collections that eventually led to the relocation of the fashion capital during the 60s.

One French designer whose simple paired down designs had also caught the spirit of the era was Andre Courreges. Courreges opened his own fashion house in 1961, and like Pierre Cardin was inspired by the new synthetic materials available. His 1964 collection futuristic, space-age collection featured short minimalistic dresses which fell above the knee.

In the following year Mary Quant raised the hemline even higher, and the miniskirt was born. It was an instant success, epitomising the spirit of London in the mid-60s; free, energetic, youthful, revolutionary and unconventional. The miniskirt perfectly complimented the clean cut look of The Beatles, the excitement of sexual permissiveness and the confidence of the new young woman.

Moral outrage and condemnation followed the miniskirt, as did a new market for accessories to compliment the look. Zip-up knee high boots made of stretch vinyl became available in bold primary colours, and earned the name of 'kinky boots'. As the short length of the miniskirt exposed women's legs, tights replaced stockings and became a fashion statement in their own right. Textured with ribs and patterns, or in solid clashing lurid colours, these tights made a women's legs the focus of attention, especially as the miniskirt got progressively shorter throughout the decade. As the younger generation was becoming less inhibited, and more sexually promiscuous due to the advent of the pill, clothes became more overt and sexual. By the late 60s the public's voracious appetite for new exciting fashions was satisfied with the miniskirt and minidress made of PVC see-through fabrics and loose crochet materials, which now made undergarments an important new feature in fashion.

left Mary Quant with partner Alexander Plunket-Greene at their Knightsbridge branch of Bazaar

Ironically the full sexuality of the miniskirt during the 60s was somewhat diluted by its sickly sweet school-girl packaging. As London became the centre of fashion it also was recognised as an industry catering almost exclusively to young girls between the ages of 15 and 20. The ideal pubescent figure shape being promoted in the fashion magazines and on the catwalks at the time contributed to this phenomenon. The image was skinny and androgynous, and was epitomised by the most famous model of the era, Twiggy. In 1966, every young girl aspired to be 17 year old Twiggy with her short boyish hairstyle, pale lips and beanpole figure. Girls copied her heavily mascaraed eyelashes to capture the 'doe-eyed' little girl look, and when dressed in a simple little miniskirt achieved the appearance of an overgrown schoolgirl. When they also struck the fashionable gawky 'broken-limb' pose they seemed to resemble shop dolls or mannequins.

By 1966 London had become the place to be. British pop music was thought to be the best, and so was British fashion, thanks to Mary Quant and other talented young designers. The excitement of London life was brilliantly conveyed by the new breed of street-wise fashion photographers like David Bailey and Terrence Donovan. They were at the centre of the London 'scene' and were up to date on fashion trends and social changes, which they captured in their distinctive fashion photographs. They shot the dramatic new fashions at equally dramatic angles and viewpoints accentuating the hip, pop-art qualities of the new styles. They photographed models in minidresses against recognisable London scenes, such as Tower Bridge, Red Double Decker Buses, Carnaby Street and the King's Road, or thoroughbred British sportscars casually parked in a Chelsea mews as backdrops for fashion which all helped to promote London as the swinging city that it was.

Swinging London was portrayed in all the popular fashion magazines of the time, such as *Nova*, *Queen* and *Vogue*, alongside the latest clothes, make-up, hairstyles and accessories. Another venue for teenagers to see the latest fashion trends was on television. To capture the ever expanding youth market, broadcasters started producing weekly pop-music programmes, such as *Ready Steady Go* and *The Beat*. These shows featured the pop idols of the day, and the latest fashion trends as well. Young viewers were able to get a weekly fashion update by noting what the host of the show and its live audiences were wearing.

The 'swinging 60s' carried on through to the end of the decade, with the popularity of the miniskirt still strong. Fashion designers created some novel, quite extreme variations in order to keep the excitement alive. Paco Rabanne launched his plastic chain mail mini in 1966, then came the ultimate in throw-away clothes, the paper minidress. Despite this inventiveness, the miniskirt length did eventually fall out of fashion.

A despondency was creeping over society due to the futileness of the Vietnam War. The future now looked less positive, and fashion became slightly nostalgic. In response, hemlines plummeted down to the ankle in 1969. This became known as the 'Maxi', much associated with the London designer label Biba, the longest length style since 1914.

Twiggy, the original dolly bird and the face of the Swinging 60s London scene – and built for the miniskirt

During the mid to late 70s a revival of London fashion occurred, known as the Punk movement. The miniskirt was revived, with female rock stars such as Debbie Harry wearing miniskirts on stage. Punk fashions had their roots in fetish and fantasywear, which was the look sold in Vivienne Westwood and Malcolm McLaren's shop SEX. The mini was now reincarnated in black leather, PVC, or in red tartans like the bondage trousers punk boys were wearing. When these skirts were worn with ripped fish-net tights, the mini took on a cheap trashy overtone which suited the 'don't care' attitude which was meant to offend.

Punks were anti-fashion motivated, and strived to create their own unique outfits, avoiding mainstrem trends which were considered bourgeois, over-indulgent and bland. Soon fashion designers created their own punk-inspired collections, which ultimately became mainstream fashions themselves.

The punk era revived the miniskirt, and also revealed its potential sexiness. The mid-1980s saw women becoming more confident about their bodies, heralding a return to the more womanly figure, and away from the adolescent androgyny of the 1960s. The miniskirt was incorporated into chic business suits for women, either in archetypal pinstripes or jewel-coloured wools as part of the 1980s power dressing outfit. Miniskirts were no longer considered just a pop garment for teenagers, but became an assertive statement for sophisticated long-legged thirty-something career women who were in total control of their single lives.

Elements of 70s punk fashion are still visible today. The clothes of active environmentalists or new age travellers combine a 'punk look' fused with hippie styling, renamed 'grunge'. The miniskirt element of 70s punk fashion has featured in a more sexy urban post-punk look which appeared in the early 1990s. This female warrior look was sexy but tough, and usually consisted of a miniskirt with a short cropped T-shirt, thick tights and combat boots complimented with body-piercing jewellery. This style was also popularised in 'Manga' style comic books like *Tank Girl* and more recently in cult video games like *Tomb Raider*. The miniskirt has become part of the female attitude referred to as 'girl power', heavily promoted by the all-girl band The Spice Girls.

The miniskirt is here to stay, demonstrated by confident young women of the 80s and 90s. Today the miniskirt is still heavily featured on catwalks and in fashion magazines, reinvented and shorter than ever. Now known as the 'micro-mini' for obvious reasons, other contemporary names for it are the 'pelmet' or 'bondage skirt'. Whatever you call it, the miniskirt is still synonymous with Mary Quant and the 'swinging 60s'.

left From British *Vogue*, September 1997, a woolen mini-dress by Yves Saint Laurent for Rive Gauche

far left A minidress as cool office wear from British *Vogue*, October 1990

above left Top designer Thierry Mugler pays homage to the classic mini

above right Modern mini fashion from a 90s Vivienne Westwood collection

11 beautiful people – the hippies

11

'The 60s were a great time to be young', is the often repeated phrase. With the post war boom and jobs for everyone, the young had money in their pockets, and provocative ideas to put on the map. It was a period of rapid change, and youth took over with energy and iconoclasm. Anything conformist was regarded with suspicion' and in art, fashion and lifestyle innovation and daring were the key words. In 1965 Kenneth Tynan, theatre critic, uttered the word 'fuck' for the first time on British television and when David Bailey married Catherine Deneuve he subverted normal wedding attire arriving in a light blue sweater and light green corduroy trousers. There was a feeling that anything was possible.

But as the 60s progressed the early optimism of the 'youthquake' began to wane, and the naive optimism which had characterised the early years gave way to more troubled times. The turning point came in the mid 60s as America became heavily involved in the Vietnam war. As the war became more intense and costly with American casualties rising steadily, it caused unrest in the US and gave the young a rare political focus. Young people were horrified by the images of war brought into their home via television and soon began to protest. Military service for US males was compulsory, and young people showed their opposition to the war by the symbolic burning of draft cards, and at protests culminating in the famous march on Washington in 1969.

Unable to come to terms with such seemingly senseless killing perpetrated against a backdrop of Western affluence, groups of young people were detaching themselves from mainstream consumer society and creating their own culture. The clean cut image of optimism of the early 60s turned to a home-grown and unkempt escapism.

The hippie movement originated in the Haight Ashbury district of San Francisco and, in rejecting Western materialism and its conspicuous consumerism, looked back with nostalgia to a rural idyll (although most of the hippies lived in urban cities). During the 60s the East was mythologised and seen as a spiritual ideal. As the price of long haul travel decreased, the hippie trail to the East began. Afghanistan and India became fashionable destinations and people began to adopt eastern religions like Buddhism and cults like Hare Krishna with their anti-materialistic philosophies. Fashion went ethnic, so as well as eulogising third world lifestyles they also began to adopt their dress.

Along the streets of Haight Ashbury, hippies could be seen wearing their multi coloured kaftans or afghan coats over fringe tasselled dresses, flat leather sandals, a headband copied straight from the American Indian or a pair of scruffy flared jeans. According to the media stereotype they greeted each other with a flower – a pseudo symbol of peace – and spent their time in drugged out contemplation of their navels.

What had started off for many as an ethical movement by a few die-hard individuals in America soon became a worldwide phenomenon influencing lifestyles and creating the mainstream fashion of the late 60s. All you had to do was grow your hair long, stick a finger up at the Establishment and you were on your way.

This was a form of anti-fashion, fashion as revolt. It was untidy and spontaneous and radically different from the chirpy neatness of the early years of the decade. The futuristic fashions (influenced by America's and Russia's space race) of the previous few years, with their clean cut asymmetric designs in plastic and other unusual materials, were rejected in favour of a romanticised past.

The hippie look was an ensemble of often contrasting sources put together in a totally haphazard way. As the hippie fashion broke away from the confines of San Francisco, kids would trawl antique stores for second hand ethnic wear. The ubiquitous blue jeans (a symbol of classless clothing) were often bought in army surplus stores, which would then be individualised with patchwork, studs or even tie dye. Long hair was a must, and anyone who wanted to rebel – and many who didn't – grew their hair.

When the tag goes on it will read NUPRON MODULIZED™ RAYON

Charles Santore

Nupron Modulized rayon lives! It does the knit bit like it's never been done before. It breathes life into blends, textures and colors. It inspires freedom in styling and dressing. It gives comfort and carefreeness wherever it goes. In short, it promises you the world. So don't let it pass you by. C'mon out in Nupron Modulized rayon. Live like you've never lived before.

Nupron Modulized rayon, a product of I-R-C Fibers Division, Midland-Ross, is made from highly purified and specialized grades of chemical cellulose produced by ITT Rayonier Incorporated, a subsidiary of International Telephone & Telegraph Corporation, New York, N.Y.

previous page Hippie-inspired body painting, from *Vogue* July 1966

right A hippie image ironically used to advertise a man-made fibre giving 'freedom in living and dressing'

Colour and exuberance in fashion was everywhere, influenced by many styles, from the American Indian to the romantic gypsy. As long as it was anti-modern it was OK. The newly established boutiques from the early 60s soon began to stock lacy blouses and fringed shawls, cheese cloth tops, velvet and frock coats, and old military 'Sgt. Pepper' jackets for men. Boutiques such as I was Lord Kitchener's Valet or Grannie Takes A Trip, (both in London) reflected the sartorial anarchy of the times with their bright riotous designs. Places like the Ethnic Emporium in London sold harem dresses in exotic silks, skirts and waistcoats made out of fringed suede and and a multitude of colourful bead necklaces.

Hippie woman reacted against the dolly bird image of the early 60s, which, with the arrival of the mini skirt, had been designed to free the young woman from sexual stereotyping, but with its thigh revealing length (often referred to as a pelmet as it was so short) confined her in a look which struck directly at the male's libido. Although the mini continued throughout the 60s, often worn extremely short under a long coat, a lot of women who leaned sartorially to the hippie ideal favoured the new long skirt length being popularised by Biba and other designers.

Ironically, the 'anti-fashion' posturing of the hippie movement was soon taken out of the communes and onto the catwalk, as designers turned the hippie style into the next essential fashion look. Flower Power was responsible for the 'handmade' look which took off in a big way, and top designers were soon showing embroidered and patchwork waistcoats in their collections. The 'beautiful people' who hung out at the trendy clubs and venues like Andy Warhol's factory in New York were soon spotted in a scruffy afghan over a Christian Dior gypsy dress. Hippie chic was the new thing in town and everyone wanted a piece of it.

Fashion teams were jetting off to Bali and India on exotic fashion shoots featuring girls lazing on sandy beaches, with brown skin and wearing the new crocheted bikini. The pages of the visually arresting *Nova* magazine were a cacophony of colour, showing models looking like creatures from another age and another continent, and a long way from the sandals-and-brown-rice culture of the original 'flower children'.

above The August 1969 *Nova* carried this picture by Jonvelle of the Christian Dior gypsy look

left From a feature in *Nova*, March 1968, describing how Flower Power brought a handmade look into fashion, the photograph by Duffy

By 1967 and the 'summer of love' the hippie philosophy of self expression and inner freedom had been taken up by many who felt free to do and wear what they wanted, and abandoned social convention. Everything tried to subvert the prevailing bourgeois values and 'Peace and Love' were the buzz words of an era striving for an apolitical ethos. Experimentation was everywhere. These were the years of the counter culture, and anarchic new ideas were being shown in art, furniture design and literature. Much went underground and people staged impromptu 'happenings' and 'love ins'. In London it was the era of *Oz* magazine, founded in 1967, with its hard-to-read psychedelic typography and controversial 'free love, free drugs' articles.

Some die-hard radicals abandoned the metropolis altogether, and armed with drugs and ideals set up home in rural communes. Living off the land, they would eke out a living making jewellery and handmade clothes to sell to their neighbouring hippie friends.

Designers caught onto this 19th Century rural preoccupation. Laura Ashley created the 'milk maid' look, with high necked dresses in pretty floral designs, more suited to a backwoods community in rural America than posing down the King's Road, London.

Although the 60s has often been criticised for its naive belief that free love and marijuana would solve the world's problems, there was a lot of creative activity which led to permanent social change. People felt free to break down taboos; the woman's movement, civil and gay rights all started in the 60s, leading to a more liberal society.

Sexual stereotypes were being broken down and 'freelove' was on the agenda for those who wanted it. All you needed was a joint of marijuana and orgiastic fulfilment was yours. Men and women began to look alike with unisex jeans and long hair, and 'You can't tell the men from the women these days' was the refrain of the older generation who felt increasingly alienated by the young.

Experimenting with gender was part of the revolution. As women took up the banner for sexual equality, men began to reject the 50s ideal of muscular machismo. The old mores of what constituted male dress were broken down and men flirted with less obvious masculine looks. They began to experiment with the feminine side of their nature and the peacock was reborn. Pop stars such as Donovan, Jim Morrison and Mick Jagger, with their soft facial features, were not shy to exploit the inherent camp possibilities. When Mick Jagger came on stage with his theatrical movements and pouting lips, questions were raised about his sexual preferences. But this just added fuel to the fire, and when he appeared at the 1969 Hyde Park concert wearing what appeared to be a woman's dress, the rebellion seemed complete.

right A 1967 promotional postcard for a US concert by Jefferson Airplane with typical 'psychedelic' typography

Sunday, 2 p.m. - 10 p.m.—Benefit for Berkeley Strike Committee with Jefferson Airplane, Quicksilver

Yves Saint Laurent – the doyen of the rich set who spent months with his chic friends at his exotic retreat in Marrakesh – created a collection for the dandyish male. He introduced velvet jackets, printed silk shirts, safari suits, kaftans and chain belts. Men would parade around, a cross between 19th Century dandies and scruffy hippies. Outfits became more outlandish with swashbuckling boots, brightly coloured jackets and fey neck scarves worn under delicate silk shirts. Young men with their hair down to their shoulders would pose in places like the King's Road or Carnaby Street in London wearing tight-fitting brightly coloured velvet trousers with flouncy shirts, complete with ruffles and waist coats.

It has been said that if you remembered the 60s, you weren't there, and indeed much of the late 60s was, for many, spent in a haze of drug-induced euphoria. The use of LSD (acid) was a powerful influence on ideas and dress. Discovered as a recreational drug by the late Harvard academic Timothy Leary, he began to publicise its mind expanding properties, and soon this powerful hallucinogenic drug was taken by hundreds of thousands of young people around the world.

By 1967, if you were groovy you were tripping on acid, and chanting Leary's mantra 'to tune in turn on and drop out'. Helped by the loosening affects of the drug people experimented with their lifestyles in the belief that they were on the road to a greater awareness and understanding. Fuelled by the sensory experience of acid and its ability to distort the senses, create hallucinations and vivid colours, people in the arts and other intellectual fields firmly believed that acid would expand the mind's awareness and unleash new creativity.

The psychedelic explosion was born, and vivid swirling patterns were everywhere from furniture design, album covers to fashion. The graphic revolution typified in posters for pop concerts, album covers like Cream's 'Disraeli Gears' and the almost-impossible-to-read pages of magazines like *Oz* and *International Times* summed up the era visually.

Psychedelia was strongly influenced by pop stars, who progressed new sounds in music vastly different from the happy beat songs of the early 60s. Psychedelic music was a rougher experimental mixture of many styles of music, with a measured dose of drug-induced special effects. Musicians like Jimmy Hendrix and Eric Clapton brought amazing techniques to bear on free-wheeling open-ended improvisation, while Bob Dylan, the Beatles and others took their lyric writing talents to new heights certainly under the influence, if not always the direct effect, of mind-expanding drugs. All, of course, was considered a bad influence on society.

left Guitarist Jimi Hendrix reclining in full hippie regalia in a portrait by Terence Donovan

Like everything, fashion became another form of self expression and responded to the psychedelic phase by introducing vivid, bold colours with flower prints on velvet skin tight trousers and dresses with abstract patterns in acid colours.

In this 'anything goes' culture, Psychedelia soon merged with Flower Power, and young men and women would pose in brightly coloured tunics, shirts over striped trousers or baggy jeans, and Afghan coats were worn with frilly shirts and brightly coloured bell bottoms. No one cared, the idea was to get groovy and do your own thing, or were they just too 'out of it' to know what was going on.

Psychedelia like hippie became high fashion, and *Vogue* showed models in various wacky poses wearing the designs of top designers. Flower prints on velvet fabrics were fashionable, and Emilio Pucci, the Italian fashion designer became famous for his acid coloured clothes especially using blues and greens.

Like many of the designers of the time who were experimenting with different types of design techniques, Zandra Rhodes became famous for her innovative use of print design and kitsch fantasy. Her materials were designed with American pop art, comic strips, lipsticks, teddy bears, hands and designs of knitting stitches. Like much of the hippie fashion she based her designs on travel and would create a collection with North American Indian shawls, Japanese prints or anything that meant a departure from the usual and normal.

In 1969, half a million hippies gathered at the Woodstock rock festival. It became a symbol of Flower Power and peace and love, but also marked the beginning of the decline. As the 60s drew to an end the euphoria began to turn ugly. Instead of bright ideas from mind expanding drugs all there was were drug casualties: Janis Joplin, Jim Morrison and Jimi Hendrix died in their twenties from drug and drink excess.

The 60s bubble was beginning to burst. In Britain the pound was devalued and in 1968 Paris was taken under siege by the student riots which caused copycat behaviour. Students everywhere staged sits ins in universities, and the London School of Economics had to be closed. Race riots were escalating and in the same year John F Kennedy, Martin Luther King and Robert Kennedy were assassinated. By the time the oil crisis struck in the early Seventies the Swinging Sixties were over.

Although there will probably never be such an exciting era again, some of the ideals and ideas have continued. Hippie culture with its rejection of western materialism is seen in the 90s New Age Traveller living in renovated buses and caravans and attempting to live off the land. Dressed in colourful clothes and jeans, like the hippies they reject pigeonholing fashions and spend their days railing against 'money grabbing society.'

Similarly the drug induced psychedelics was too good a trip to go away. It returned in the mid 80s with the Rave culture. This time the drug was Ecstasy and trippers would dance till dawn in their brightly coloured acid clothes, dayglo gloves and 'smiley' T shirts shouting 'Aciiid' to the monotonous beat of Acid house music.

above The new psychedelia of the
90s – a teenager at a 'rave' club

left Anna Sui designed this lacey
see-through hippie-inspired dress
for Spring 1993

far left The spectacular fabric
prints used by Emilio Pucci were
famous for their acid-colour impact

12

studio 54 – club chic

12

In the 1970s discoteques were spectacular arenas, carnivals of excess, places to live out a fantasy and to be seen doing so, stylishly, just for the night. The senses were satiated by effects such as strobe lighting, dry ice, sensurround, multi-media shows, and amplified by the materials worn by the disco dancers: spandex, lurex, lycra, rayon, gold lame, dazzling rhinestones, sequins, diamante, body glitter and gloss. The pleasure-seeker left the banality of his everyday existence, discharged all inhibitions and submitted himself to the rituals of the disco sect.

Disco started as an underground movement in about 1973. By the late 70s it had exploded as a global phenomenon. New York's Studio 54 resembled in many ways Tony Manero's stomping ground in the film *Saturday Night Fever*. However it was, in many ways, different from the local neighbourhood disco and took its inspiration both from the discos that Steve Rubell, its flamboyant owner, had run previously, and the gay nightclubs in down-town New York. Studio 54 was not just about music and dancing but more about a self-conscious decadent sensibility; a desire to see and be seen, behaving badly.

From its beginning Studio 54 was the wildest and most debauched of night clubs, constantly exposed in the media for its scandalous events. Rubell, who opened the nightclub in an abandoned TV theatre on West 54th Street in the Spring of 1977, established an exciting and addictive pleasure palace where club-goers could pose and hang out as well as overindulge in abundant sex and drugs. Once you were a regular you belonged to a wild-living, dysfunctional family.

The club was designed for effortless people-watching. Posing took place in the huge theatrical space of the main disco where a balcony, stage, dance floor and silver screen kept exhibitionists on view. Sex and drugs were consumed in the basement and on the balcony whilst celebrities idled in the VIP lounge. The DJ in his booth, creator of the disco ambiance, multiplied the sensual and erotic layers of the disco sound by engineering a seamless fusion of tracks.

previous page John Travolta in *Saturday Night Fever*, the 1977 film that stereotyped the 70s disco boom

right Studio 54 on the club's first birthday, which celebrated Elizabeth Taylor's 50th the same night in 1978

right Liza Minnelli and Russian ballet star Mikhail Baryshnikov on the dance floor at Studio 54

right Andy Warhol watches Debbie Harry and Truman Capote dancing at a Studio 54 *Interview* magazine party

The door policy was strict but democratic; contemporary icons, freaks and beautiful people were invited in and those who did not fit into the scene were kept out. An elite clique known as the glitterati, members of which were drawn from the artistic and entertainment aristocracies, kept the club in the newspaper headlines.

The guest list included fashion designers such as Halston and Yves Saint Laurent, actresses such as Elizabeth Taylor and Liza Minelli (who together with Halston was elected king and queen of the club), artists and writers such as Andy Warhol and Truman Capote, dancers such as Nureyev and Baryshnikov – all participated in the excessive hedonism of Studio 54. Steve Rubell organised themed nights when debauchees would put on fancy dress. For her birthday party, Halston had Bianca Jagger dressed in white and gold, and led through the club on a white horse by a black man who was attired only in a dusting of gold glitter. The philosophy at the club was that anything goes, legal or illegal.

The door policy dictated that club goers had to be famous, or look original to ensure that they stood out from the crowd. The mixed white, black, straight and gay crowd could choose from a plethora of styles from past and contemporary subcultures and cult styles. The glamourous drag queens, replicas of Marilyn; leather clad gays, exposing sado-masochistically bound buttocks and torsos; girls draped in 40s and 50s vamp gowns; label cognoscenti dressed in Halston, Gucci and Fiorucci. Latin disco dancers; keep fit fanatics and funksters dressed as characters and extras from an epic film, taking part in an erotic display and continuing the disco tradition of dressing up to go dancing, but with an ironic knowingness, all part of the self-conscious plundering of styles.

It is this relative freedom with which people experimented with individual fashion fantasies which perhaps distinguishes the 70s from earlier eras. Throughout the 70s fashion buccaneers could identify with any style, take it out of context and live fantasy lifestyles. Studio 54's house chic condensed the multifarious styles and saw the culmination of an extensive process of cross fertilization between the street, pop and haute couture.

If it were possible to reduce the tastes of the 1970s to an essence, with this excess of borrowings of styles from the dressing up box of the past and present, then it could be identified as a decade of camp sensibility. The styles that were looted; the icons that were idolised: art nouveau, art deco, the pre-Raphaelites, Berlin during the Weimar republic, glamour queens of the inter-war years like Garbo and Dietrich, were interpreted at face value but also because they in themselves embodied the aesthetics of camp.

Alongside this ability to choose from a range of styles regardless of the context a more serious fashion aesthetic existed. The androgynous clothes many women chose to wear, expressed the burgeoning women's movement and their desire to be taken more seriously as they entered the work force on a more equal footing. Revlon's Charlie Girl strides across the 70s urban environment in several variations of men's clothing: the trouser suit, the boiler suit and dungarees. Japanese deconstructive fashion reflected other movements in art, land art and brutalism in architecture. But even these serious fashion statements could be appropriated and worn with a camp awareness. Studio 54 provided an exhibition space to display this awareness, choosing style over content. Disco was anti-serious; the camp aesthete par excellence.

Studio 54 represented the twilight of an era of 'sexual liberation, over indulgence and decadence'. The sexual revolution may have been discussed ad infinitum in the 1960s, but it could be argued that it actually happened and exploded in the 1970s, especially in increasingly jaded ways. The chic new sexual conventions of the day denied that a person's sexuality could be neatly classified. In the early 70s Bowie and Jagger had disturbed the sexual stereotypes and high society experimented with the endorsement of bisexuality as a lifestyle choice. Studio 54 was not a place where 'boy meets girl' but a place where sexual decadence reigned, underpinned by a homoerotic aesthetic which continued the rituals of New York's gay scene. There are plenteous stories of indiscriminate sex, abandoned drug taking and ejaculation contests taking place in the infamous basement.

Disco cult 'looks' blurred the boundaries between masculine and feminine, a process which had been initiated at the beginning of the decade as a challenge to received views of masculinity and femininity. Bianca and Mick Jagger's wedding suits (1971) by Yves Saint Laurent, expressed an interchangeable sexuality. The designer was a key figure in the 1970s indulgence with decadent fashion, asserted in both his designs and lifestyle. His ubiquitous 'smoking' epitomised this decadence. It was borrowed from a masculine context thus conveying an ambiguous sexual message. In Helmut Newton's 1975 photograph a lean model, dressed in a low cut 'smoking', wanders the night time streets, cigarette held insouciantly. The black and white of the photo suggests a low, down town area through which the woman strolls with detachment. Woman masquerading as man. Saint Laurent took other references during the 70s, the hippy look from the late 60s, glam rock, theatre design, a Russian peasant style, Carmen and Morocco and produced pret a porter and couture versions of these themes.

left Andy Warhol, Calvin Klein, Brooke Shields and Steve Rubell at the re-opening of Studio 54 in 1981

right An early celebrated example of 70s sexually ambiguous dress, Mick and Bianca Jagger in their 1971 wedding suits by Yves Saint Laurent

above Designer and Studio 54 regular Halston with models wearing his creations in March 1975, and (opposite) some of his designs

Men could assume ultra masculine disguises. The skinhead/gang look which had largely disappeared by the early 70s was taken up by the gay subculture and crossed with the S&M based leather gear look. A toned down funk/pimp look, made popular in blaxploitation movies, became the uniform of disco groovers and influenced *pret a porter*. The serious army look bought from army surplus stores in the early part of the decade, which symbolised the student dissatisfaction with the Vietnam war, gave way to a high fashion, urbane statement. The broad shouldered military/navy look with epauletts, medals, kepis and khaki in expensive materials had nothing to do with demonstrating against the status quo and everything to do with posing. The appropriation of male stereotypes was initiated by gay culture which turned them into methods of group identification that were then taken up in different ways by heterosexual style makers.

Opportunities existed in the 70s for both men and women to mimic ultra feminine guises. In the early 70s there had been a move towards a retro vampish glamour from the inter war years. Hair was rolled back and to the side throughout the decade, and in a variety of fabric cuts from the 30s and 40s dresses stressed the body. The materials used – chiffon, crepe de chine and jersey – looked back to previous fashion eras. The clothes were photographed by Helmut Newton and Guy Bourdin, using models posed like mute mannequins and conveying an ambiguous sexuality. Retro shops sprang up in the major capitals and the retro chic style was copied by designers such as Barbara Hulaniki and Norma Kamali. This early 70s vamp style was revived in the late 70s when the female sophisticate and drag queen took up the key details – witty little hats, net veils, lace, spindly court shoes, strappy gold sandals, kohled eyes, kitsh accessories and fetishised them.

Designers who catered for night time revellers emphasised a rich feminine sensuality by offering women ways to shine and look glamourous in nightclubs such as Studio 54. Skin tight satin trousers, footless tights, shorts, leotards, split skirts and strapless cocktail dresses revealed bronzed glossy limbs. The sensuality of materials used, transparent fabrics, lace, cashmere, suede, leather, velvet and silk in opulent colours or black emphasised the body's erotic zones. Make-up emphasised the sexual message with vibrant shiny and glossy colours and a wet look on skin and lips. Designers, such as Halston, Norma Kamali and Sue and Perry Ellis even got involved in designing specifically for the discotheque. Halston designed outfits for his friend Liza Minelli to go clubbing in and Norma Kamali used spandex to design bright coloured disco gear.

If there was a rule that unified all these disparate looks it was to a redefining of the body itself. Experimentation with body shapes was achieved through clothes and through the new keep fit craze. A lean and thin silhouette for women was prescribed which was to be achieved through diet and exercise, especially the new crazes of jogging and disco dancing. Tanning was also encouraged 'rich girls of course are brown all the time, all the year round'. American designers such as Calvin Klein were recognised as the leaders of this new look that emphasised health and natural beauty. Their clothes were simple, elegant and adapted to modern active lives. Disco wear was influenced by the keep fit craze; waiters at

Studio 54 dressed in satin gym shorts designed to turn the punters of both sexes on. Fiorucci also designed clothes with a fitness theme.

There was a feeling in the 70s that people were living in decadent times; a feeling that traditional relations between families and couples had changed irretrievably due to post war youth, gender and sexual explosions reaching a critical point. Many felt a sense of confusion, that society had changed too drastically, that 'a privileged minority were behaving appallingly' and were experimenting in dangerous ways. Studio 54 symbolised in the minds of many this orgiastic dissipation, an image which the club's organisers did nothing to dispel. The club's logo was the man in the moon sniffing stars as if they were cocaine. Cocaine became the fashionable drug. It was taken by the members of the international Jet Set; 'the Beautiful People', a term popularised by the group around Andy Warhol, enduring hippies, who luxuriated in a mixture of drugs, money and beauty. And it was these people who made their way to Studio 54.

Drugs were an integral part of the fashion industry, a situation referred to in the advertisement for the new Yves Saint Laurent perfume Opium. Jerry Hall was photographed for the advertisement in Saint Laurent's apartment which had been recreated as a sensual opium den with rich exotic colours drawing attention to the apparently stupefied Hall. The double entendre of the advert's slogan stressed the drug references, *'Pour celles qui s'addonnent a Yves Saint Laurent'* ('For those that devote themselves to Yves Saint Laurent').

The Studio 54 aesthete quoted profanely in order to assert his urbanity in matters of taste and to disassociate himself from the mass, joining an elite clique which shared his tastes. It is a matter for debate as to what made this aesthete more inclined to spend time and energy on escapist nostalgia in order to be able to play with the styles of past eras. Perhaps it was the growing scepticism in modernity and the idea of future progress that made the past and the theatricality of dressing up seem inspirational. Perhaps it was the general feeling of decline during the 70s brought on by economic depression, excessive inflation, unwinnable wars and government corruption.

Tom Wolfe called the 70s the 'Me' decade. Discos epitomised the self awareness of posing, the feeling of wanting to stand out from the crowd and at the same time the importance of belonging to a scene. At the same time 70s consumer culture quickly assimilated the 70s collage of tastes in order to supply it to a mass market; any subculture could be infiltrated by anybody with only a trace of a game plan. Disco itself has been criticised as a capitalist construction, music producers making bland records to a formulaic blueprint. But any visitor to Studio 54 could not ignore the sheer scale of the hedonistic pleasures on offer. Studio 54 lasted less than two years. In 1979 due to undeclared tax receipts Rubell and his partner were forced to close the club.

What, if anything, was the club's influence on fashion and street style? In the short term, clubs took up the themed-night innovation that Rubell had made popular. In London the Embassy Club and in Paris, Le Palace, copied the Studio 54 style. New Romantics at the Blitz Club made dressing up in the inherited artifacts of pop culture a decadent rite of passage. However night life in the 80s took a very different path with acid house ravers deliberately dressing down in T-shirts, baggy trousers and trainers.

Disco's highest point coincided with an increasing cross fertilization of ideas between American and European designers, with a movement towards an international mass market – American fashion started to be noticed in Europe.

Detractors of the 70s have condemned it as the Bad Taste decade but in its kitshness lies its attraction. The 70s has become a cult decade. Itself the borrower of styles from previous eras it has been quoted and revived numerous times; its competing styles alluring in their referentiality, original in their conventionality. It paved the way for a continued appropriation of the past. 70s discos, 70s fashions are still enjoyed with the same camp self-consciousness as they were the first time around.

right A 1995 shot by Nick Knight showing the influence of 70s glam and glitter as retro style 20 years on

anti-fashion and punk couture

13

Fashion has always had its social conscience and can be the perfect vehicle for powerful political messages, from the iconisation of Che Guevara's portrait to the anti-war sloganeering of Katharine Hamnett's T shirts. But the truly unexpected that flies in the face of fashion itself can carry an equally powerful signal as the blatantly written message.

Anti-fashion is by definition the opposite of fashion, so if it exists, it should be different every time fashion changes. But its rules stay the same because what it actually represents is all negative – anarchy, destruction of order and the instigation of chaos. And there is one character who embodies all the nihilism of this cause, all the ignorance of one who could dispense with the prizes of civilisation and hate the *haut monde* enough to mock it by wearing its clothes, its badges of status and excellence, in a disrespectful manner; the yob, the hooligan, the punk.

In 1976-77 a smoother and smoother veneer was being painted over everything in pop culture. Music in particular was becoming less and less spontaneous and more formulaic, stadium-oriented rock acts like Pink Floyd and Led Zeppelin were laying track over track on overproduced albums, and their media images were increasingly airbrushed and pathologically neat and geometric.

In response came a phenomenon seemingly out of nowhere that was so potent that most streetstyle as we know it has never been the same since, the core ethos of which still has a dedicated following over 20 years later. It was Punk. It was deliberately amateur, inarticulate and self-consciously working class, though as with many revolutions, its participants were often surprisingly middle class. Cynics rather than architects of any utopia, their cry to arms was 'no future' and bands like the Sex Pistols sang 'Pretty Vacant', not songs of revolution but emptiness.

The tribal nature of the dress has been much commented on. The defiance and the sartorial elements do correspond to the concept within Punk of being in a pack, which propelled the classic elements of punk – the kilt, the bondage trousers, the Doc Martens, the SEX T-shirts alluding to menstruation, faeces and any other subject usually glossed over by polite society, the spiderweb knits and PVC or leather lavatory chains and day-glo mohicans – into a cult status. It was this feeling that shock tactics must be used to get society to acknowledge the innate violence and brutality underlying the niceties. Slogans like 'we are all prostitutes', and the idea of commercially selling clothes catering to fetishists coming from speciality companies in a brown paper envelope seemed shocking then, but now seems merely interesting as a social phenomenon. In a sense, it had to happen, the haze of testosterone-crazed heavy metal fashions and inane disco hits was a cry for help in itself. The only thing these style politicos really suffered from was boredom.

Art school Situationists latched on to a romantic view of rock'n'roll as an anthem of disenchanted proletarian youth. The apathy towards the Queen's Jubilee, increasing unemployment and Labour's demise made the underclass the successors of the working class heroes of the 60s boom. No future, no hippie vision for these the inheritors of the leather jacket of the true rebel, but everyone in music seemed old or insipid at the time, so they took their cue from the New York Dolls and Rocky Horror Show and made bin liners, dog collars and ripped jeans a statement of youth. Later it was hip to subvert school uniform, or appear so spectacularly boring that you looked insane, or to be covered in graffiti and safety pins. Sartorial anarchy was the ideology and its legacy has multiplied over the 20 years since with the endless permutations of punk clothing, which constantly becomes incorporated into other trends.

right Vivienne Westwood (far right) with a collection of customers at her seminal London shop SEX in 1977

Punk certainly struck a chord with French Intellectos immediately. Their admiration for the movement produced sometimes laughable cross-channel versions with twee hoppity skip songs and coy names, but they helped enshrine the cult to such an extent that it is still taken very seriously in France. Essays and dissertations were written about it at universities, long before we came to value or eulogise it.

The movement's originators, Vivienne Westwood and Malcolm McLaren, were coming from this philosophical bent too, although, they were cunning enough to express it in inarticulate terms at first. Westwood has gone on to prove further still, that she is absolutely in tune with the needs of fashion; it needs art, it needs tradition and it serves as valid social comment. She has entertained us with her wacky ideas and collections with names like 'Britain must go Pagan' and 'Pirates,' we have loved her mini-crini and tweed puffball skirts, but shuddered at the thought of wearing them. Until, that is, the mainstream picked them up and then the originals were recognised for the brilliant and brave ideas they really were.

Corsets and Pirates are themes that run on and on. In fact, the rag-picking retro themes in top couture today are rooted in what Westwood was doing from the early 80s. Punks wearing the garb of the aristocracy is what it is all about. Copies of real historical clothes, corsets with Versailles pictures, 18th century men's dandy clothes for women, even her own version of Dior's New Look. She is daring, vocal and dead-on. What is so phenomenal is her love of the arguments she feels for making these clothes, and her understanding not only of tailoring, so that her Harris Tweed 40s suits actually flatter the figure and feel comfortable, but her knowledge of the impact the shapes and colours made in their own time.

Westwood's theme of pirates was so clever from the start, because it gave the wearer the same sort of ability to intimidate as Punk, only more authoritative, because of its historical awareness. The almost frightening way a pirate would take a thing that struck his fancy and wear, say a rich man's hat, with ottoman trousers, a dead man's frock coat or even a peg leg. Because he was obviously the sort of person who had stolen it, who did not have the right to wear it so blatantly, so triumphantly, he made anyone who encountered him wonder about his intentions and what he would do to them. The female revolutionary, who took the aristocrat's wig as he went to the guillotine and wore it with her servants gown, maybe gave off a look of defiance, sexual ambiguity and dangerous power, too. Or was she a 20th Century creation?

left From the Paris Summer collections of 1994, Gaultier's body-piercing echoes of 70s punk

far left Part of the original Bromley Contingent, the original punks who hung around SEX, including (left) the much-photographed Cat Woman

Jean Paul Gaultier adopted the main elements of punk and made them into Gallic fashion on the edge. The major creations from his original collection were resuscitated in the Winter 97/98 Freeman's catalogue, a mass-market UK mail order outlet, but with his skirt trousers for men and his unusual visual comments on sexual differences, he was able to become a big seller in the UK because he understood the underlying need for challenging clothes and why it was happening at that moment. Skirts and trousers worn together raise enough sexual questions to show that anything normal is ultimately questionable. The skirt and bra can only belong to women, yet women can wear men's clothes and look fascinating. As to why this is, it appears to be simply an idee fixe, but JPG forced us to confront these issues without words.

JPG had a major triumph with his Madonna clothes and pointy breasts, the pinstripe suit with the big old fashioned satin bra with no give, worn without a shirt or blouse. Only the supremely confident would wear these clothes though, and it took a freedom from the strictures of ordinary work to have the occasion to. These were clothes for rich marginales.

His scent bottle, in an hourglass shape that represented a traditional form of female bondage, went further than Schiaparelli's Mae West silhouette for her 'Shocking' perfume that appeared in the 1930s. It suggested that sexual power was itself a kind of bondage or hard work as well as the obvious, exciting connotations. The antithesis of the norm in perfume advertising, the folklore is 'wear this and they'll fall at your feet'. The iconoclast now suggested that it was all artifice, the myth was false and you have to work at being a woman to every audience; lover, family or public. Female bondage and work are familiar motifs in his work; the dinky Dutch woman with plaits and spacy kitchen utensils or the omnipresent laced-up corset that becomes a packaged person in a wedding dress or Western good-time girl, the full figure being the ultimate transgression in the androgynous world of real careers.

Creating chaos out of order is the essence of change. This is why so often couture houses show such mad and exaggerated clothes on the runway. The hair and make-up is mostly influential but not copied religiously by the public. The designers know that it is an effective way to grab headlines and the broader stroke is the way to get the smaller changes through.

New romanticism, Goths, Cyberpunks, Pervs, New Agers, Grunge and other mainstream youth streetstyles, as exemplified by Cyndi Lauper and early Madonna, all carry the imprint of punk. Most youth styles today owe a huge debt to punk, as does the world of haute-couture.

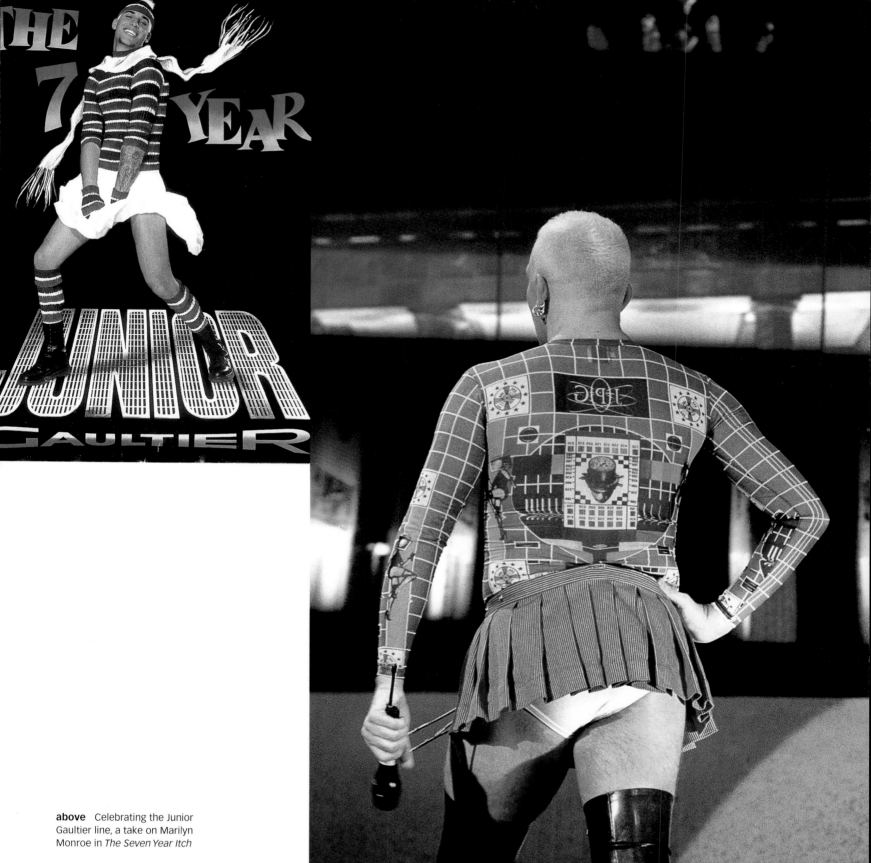

above Celebrating the Junior Gaultier line, a take on Marilyn Monroe in *The Seven Year Itch*

left Jean-Paul Gaultier's infamous 'bondage' scent bottle

right Gaultier himself, enjoying his role as a major media personality at the MTV Music Awards

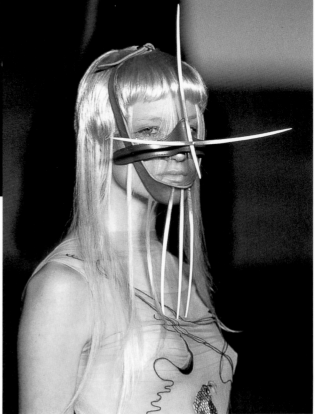

above Alexander McQueen adjusts a 'jungle collection' outfit featuring the antlers of a Thompson gazelle

right More bondage-influence inspired by early punk, from Alexander McQueen 1997

left From McQueen's degree show
collection, the much-publicised
'builder's bum' look

Forget Karl Lagerfeld's biker boots for the Princess Stephanie set. This is hard-core. Alexander McQueen's violence and ability to push boundaries has moved into more terrifying areas, because this is the punk as tyrannical designer and he really works it. His humour and the rumours only heighten its appeal. Like with the famous Sex Pistols foul-mouthing confrontation on UK TV in 1976, the press vicariously enjoy the stories of the salon seamstresses . . . terror shown by collective knitted eyebrows while they silently scream in unison, 'what will he slash next?'

The persistent rumour that he is to be sacked, the outrage over his comments about the great Givenchy 'what talent' and the 'Burke and Hare' tone of his collection last Spring. 'The police were supposedly called in to investigate the use of body parts . . .

'The fashion world was chilled . . . ' etc etc. The hype went on and on, but he has always used accessories made of fish skin and animal bone, hair and feathers. And yes, he used the huge antlers of a Thompson gazelle on the shoulders of an otherwise immaculate suit, for his jungle collection. Other features of this heavily publicised collection were parts of crocodile . . . why should crocodile just be in the shape of shoes and bags? Do they look more natural that way? The models also had dark eyes and a white belly, akin to being in the African food chain. The waist and hips were accentuated into a beautiful shape, showing sexual competition at its best. 'It's a jungle out there' was the refrain. It is crude and laughable, yet McQueen knows just how long the press tolerates a designer, even given his innovative skill and technical merit.

McQueen's Savile Row apprenticeship and the obscene messages he sewed into suit linings are legend. Yet he seems always a jump ahead structurally, as his exquisite punched leather evening dresses show. The McQueen ideal of modern clothing should create emotion and be a blend of sabotage and tradition with the beauty and the violence of the time.

Change of body shape, elongating the abdomen and an homage to the British workman 'bum cleavage' failed to impress. He was bound to be misunderstood as a working class British gay male, and the inevitable comparison with British 'builders' bum' was snickered at in the press, but he was only initiating a change that usually comes about naturally in fashion evolution. Periodically, a different body part comes under the spotlight according to factors peculiar to the era. However, not usually according to the whim of arrogant young designers.

All revolution must destroy to reconstruct, that is its nature. In order to break down the barriers, someone must ridicule those things which we hold dear, to juxtapose unlikely objects or styles together and to feel the pain of realisation that certain things that have served us well are no longer the truth. This is the nature of art and particularly of fashion, because there are institutionalised reasons for needing change. In fashion, that is the Season. It is something in the human psyche that we decorate ourselves in finery, animals are given theirs, by right. But only we have the prerogative to make sure that the criteria for ours suit our purposes, our vocabulary and our purpose and if they do not, then we must update it and if necessary, force the change.

This is what fashion has always done, but the re-invention of the past is purely 20th Century. We are, it seems, characterised by our constant looking at ourselves, examining society and its foundations and undergoing a kind of mass cultural therapy. That is what characterises this genre of fashion – it faces facts full on, warts and all, and makes a higher kind of artistic statement.

Everyone who wears it is a leader, unlike the revolution of, say, the mini skirt, which was all about following, or the hippie cult, which was escapist fantasy. Through those trends fashion briefly had us believe that we had been liberated from associated credo or class because fashion was now the territory of the young and fit, rather than the rich and idle.

The concerns of Couture and streetstyle have been symbiotic for some time now. We cannibalise cliché after cliché in an effort to explore and romanticise, play dressing up, and work at the roles that inspire us in our daily lives. But it must always be an antidote to boring, always the twist that refreshes. Punk came along just before the Japanese changed the shape of designer fashion. Change of dimensions, the tone or the message is where it really matters now in fashion, irreverence, wit and upsetting our expectations have all become priorities. Eclecticism, spontaneity and play are essential elements, but in this game, technical supremacy is crucial.

Change is more literal on the street and more bare-faced about the message, but there is a place for the grandeur and more opulent scale as the couture shows continue to show. When the haute couture mavericks do it, it can be breathtaking, so long as it is on the edge by virtue of some imaginary dread event or 'last-vestiges-of-civilisation' or a genuinely original joke. It must always be remembered that the frontiers are cerebral and dependent on universal emotion and not the hazards of manufacture and retailing. Too literal a translation and the sartorial vision is no use to your clients, too benign, like the Zandra Rhodes version of punk. No attention to the tradition you knock and your work is invalid. That is when the hunter really does become the hunted, but then, for some people, maybe that is the most terrible beauty of all.

left An Alexander McQueen outfit modelled at London Fashion Week in September 1996

designer labels
— corporate chic

During the 1980s, fashion became integral to the newly emerging concept of 'the lifestyle'. The new wealth and prosperity hyped in the media was ever-more evident throughout the decade and was a shot in the arm for all types of retailers and media in Britain, the US and elsewhere. In the UK the 'big bang' deregularisation of the stock market and an explosion in property prices, helped establish the culture of the yuppie. The making of a new *haute bourgeoisie* was in at least one respect similar to the emergence of the industrial rich in the 19th Century; the way they spent money. But this time, everyone wanted to experience everything at once, and there emerged a new puritanism and quest for order to avoid the commercial and visual chaos of the 70s. In fashion, that meant that all the teen headbangers who had played cardboard guitar to their hairy heroes in the previous decade cleaned up their act and began to live the corporate dream. The medium really did become the message and to succeed, it looked as if all you had to do was dress right and think positive. Censorious 'style police' were everywhere and it seemed you couldn't get away with just being a mogul, what you bought defined you once and for all. There was enormous wealth around, but it was spent with a corporate mentality, so that even the most exotic trophy wife appeared to be dressing not only for her man, but for boardroom approval.

The pursuit of excellence was of utmost importance in every area of life from hi-fi to holidays. But, given the immediacy of style in other areas, it is surprising just how long it took for the two major styles that began the decade to finally fuse. The ultimate look was a combination of the Thierry Mugler exaggerated Travis Banton 40s hourglass shape with the flounced peplum, that found its new muse in Alexis from *Dynasty* and the strict preppy, or Sloane image. The snappy suit was the only style statement worth making for almost 10 years and although its potency was hugely mythologised through films like *Working Girl*, *Baby Boom* and *Fatal Attraction*, where the clothes defined the personality, it took years to become the refined serious item we remember, simply because women were afraid to give up the ruffles. It went through all sorts of structural changes before 'everywoman' had the guts to wear the pared-down version and yet, by the end of the decade, it seemed indispensable, even if you were a supermarket shelf stacker and only wore your power suit in your leisure time.

American fashion came into its own on both sides of the Atlantic, the 'special relationship' between the two countries forged between the Reagans and Margaret Thatcher meant that a new aristocracy was emerging and wanted to be seen. The camera readiness of the superstars of the day, and their fantasy counterparts in soap opera, made it a unique decade. Lifestyle magazines and television programmes became the big audience pullers and advertising began to present narrative-type fashion shoots. In both *Dynasty* and the pages of *Hello!* people or characters were symbolised by their possessions, they were full of men in cowboy boots in front of an estancia, paintings and helicopters in the background, women in their boudoirs wearing lingerie, and celebrities caught off-guard with bags of shopping from Rodeo Drive. Even the *Miami Vice* series had a colour code as rudimentary as graffiti; character and objects were reduced to symbolism, you read the nature of the individual by the clothes and accessories. In fiction, clothes and designer drugs featured as the main focal point in Jay McInerney's *Bright Lights, Big City,* while Brett Easton Ellis parodies the eclectic nature of 80s cuisine, and meticulously describes the clothes of the amoral young, in *American Psycho* and *Less Than Zero*.

Diana, Princess of Wales was a major influence on fashion throughout the decade. She had the rare gift of combining aristocratic grace with the stature of a catwalk model. She championed the interests of British fashion at home and abroad and had her own unique international stage. Her style emerged over the years into a more and more sophisticated and confidently intuitive one. Having your outfit on her back was a priceless piece of publicity, but even for those who copied, she was a strong influence and a tonic to the industry. She gave hope to a whole new generation of couturiers and mainstream designers, and a new outlook to many girls who could now wear such clothes without having to be a debutante or one of the landed gentry.

The obsession with class and, in the UK, 'the Season', and the lifestyle of the rich and famous, was heightened at this time by the birth of *Hello!* magazine, the hip sociology of Peter York and Ann Barr's *Sloane Ranger* and *Preppy Handbooks*. The Season and the charity ball, hitherto the stage for aristos and insiders, became another fun day or night for the commercial meritocrat and celebrities. Hats came back in, largely due to Diana, the young girl in public life. The idea of being young in a traditional role was a myth used time and again in narrative fashion shoots and, due to the phenomenal success of mail order during the 80s, brochures and catalogues. The biggest innovation in mail order in Britain was the Next catalogue, and its Winter 88-89 edition featured young beautiful people, with children, the ultimate living accessory, in the grounds of some country house, in modern, traditional clothes. Bruce Weber created a very particular nostalgia through rose tinted glasses for Ralph Lauren, and *Vogue* constantly had photo-narratives of young things in old Hollywood in evening wear on the tennis court, or 'modern' 50s couples kissing the children goodnight on the way out to the opera. All the fantasies you could absorb on the same theme; young, rich, having it all, and for most consumers the biggest fantasy was that you'd always been that way.

left Diana, Princess of Wales, in a dress by Murray Arbeid in 1987

Ralph Lauren was quick to exploit a very key fashion arena of the 20th Century – the department store. Walk into any mall or shopping centre, go to his selling space and you were on a stage set. Try on the clothes, whatever theme, it felt right among the mahogany and real antiques. He hired a full-time team in London to hunt down old steamer trunks, leather bound books and croquet mallets, for the right ambience. For trying on blazers, white flared pants and sneakers, the wooden lined space could be an ocean liner; try on a t-back, slinky evening gown, it was a club during Prohibition. Tweed suit? OK, then it's a guest bedroom at Blenheim. His fashion was so cleverly classic 20th Century re-worked for modern times. Every fashion story of the 30s, 40s and classic American sportswear took on a certain grandeur. Even Safari scent was imbued with the spirit of *Now Voyager* and Norman Parkinson's famous aeroplane photo, by suggestion and good pictures. Gentlemanly refinement was innate in the names Polo and Dressage, implying a knowledge of good form and being an insider. But membership of this club was bought.

The department store was of utmost importance to this type of fashion distribution. Other designers, such as Versace and Dolce & Gabbana had their flagship stores as temples to their own style and 'tugboat departments' in the larger stores. Pride of place became of utmost importance in an increasingly competitive and expensive market, and in England, there was a particular cachet about American fashion too. Many sophisticates bought *Vanity Fair* for the 'American-ness' of the advertising.

Lauren's clothes also feature a concept peculiar to 1980s clothes; the logo and the emblem. A quiet revolution was going on in terms of social events; the Season and certain sports were also being stormed by the huge quota of Corporate entertainments, as reward for high flyers or, more likely, as client seduction. Fashion magazines were full of advice for the uninitiated on how to succeed and play the toffs at their own game. How to belong, how to fit in and how to look enviably rich and sophisticated. Consequently, emblems and logos were hugely popular as the buyers learned to recognise each other and approve the way it was worn. It was fun to play with their symbols and in time, manufacturers' logos overtook the genuine emblems of status.

right An aspirational room set, part of the interior of Ralph Lauren's Rhinelander store in New York

right Labels and logos become design and status symbols; here, Chanel from the 1992 collections

far right The sensational micro-bikini designed by Karl Lagerfeld for Chanel – and clearly carrying the logo – which made its appearence in 1995

Younger women in their Chanel and Hermes learned to customise their look to stay ahead. The braided jacket with jeans, the gilt chain handbag, was enlarged and corrupted by Karl Lagerfeld himself into biker gear, as the young with money became really plentiful. Couture was back with a vengeance and a large part of dressing, at least among the social X rays, was by women for other women. As in the 1940s, after dark, the hardbitten boardroom-stereotype of a woman would shed her boxy, padded shouldered jacket and slide into her ballgown. The salons of Oldfield, Bellville Sassoon, Murray Arbeid and the Emanuels (after their phenomenal success with the Princess Of Wales' wedding gown) created confections calculated to fulfil female fantasy, whatever background its wearer had come from. Charity balls abounded and fashion, free enterprise and good causes were fused to promote themselves and the wearers. Socialites began to be pictured on the tiny gilt chairs of the catwalk shows once more.

The concern for one's fitness became paramount, hence the trend for tiny exquisite portions and the obligatory membership of a gym. As women's bodies became more toned and not just thin thin, designers such as Alaia and the budget Pineapple range were everywhere. Lycra was in every daywear range, and leggings and cashmere sweaters were the perfect combination of revealing, but luxurious garb. Bodies on show, inciting lust, greed, pride, avarice and envy; fashion really was breaking the ten commandments.

High heels both accentuated authority in the daytime, whether social or corporate, and they emphasised the degree to which sexuality was expressed. Skirts became aggressively short simultaneously. Power dressing was much more masculine, and yet curiously more feminine, than the 70s career-oriented styles.

The huge prices charged for items of clothing and accessories with designer names were justified as investments. Whether it be crocodile or stamped leather, it was essential to buy the best you could. Even the jeans market became one for the connoisseur. The Financial Times even started their magazine How To Spend It on the premise of investment. Full of advertisements for expensive watches and scarves, features on couture and the best of everything in decoration, restaurants, wine and leisure activities, it extended its authority on shares and capital markets to consumer items. Accessories proliferated, and women were known to snip off Chanel buttons in the shops to tack them onto inferior copies at home. Logos were everywhere, on jeans, jackets, sports shirts and cars. A New York teen group, The Beastie Boys went one stage further and wore car logos round their necks on thick gold chains, like black rappers, inspiring a million more thefts as the irony caught on.

Calvin Klein's clothes fitted perfectly with the investment theme. His minimalist style represented a no-nonsense chic, technical skill and workmanship, and total dedication to modernism. The muted palette and discipline required to wear it properly also appealed to the very discerning and moneyed customer. But it wasn't just money, it was and is an understanding. Klein himself coined a delicious oxymoron when he claimed it was 'couture for the *prêt-a-porter* market'. Many designers made their clothes in understated luxury fabrics, with the workmanship assured to be the best, even though the garments were often made in third world countries using cheap labour.

It is a look for independent women, there are no themes or associations, or logos. The shapes were much imitated in the 80s by the whole garment industry, and ultimately it made the fashion business realise that they had scored a massive own goal. The classic item was not often replaced, and its simplicity made it easy to copy by definition. This would eventually provoke another *faux pas* known as grunge in a desperation to cast off the look of obscene wealth and get into Prada's 'cleaning lady' outfits or Anna Sui, in order to regain credibility. It only succeeded in alienating buyers. Lean mean fashion machines dominated the 80s fashion pages. In truth few were truly involved in it, fewer still got the bounty, but no-one would refuse to play the game until doing so actually *became* the game in the early 90s.

Men and women were better groomed than they had been in years. Services like Sock Shop and Tie Rack put an end to any excuse for scruffiness on the way to work. Colour co-ordination was of utmost concern, women simplified their wardrobes and the tyranny of black, beige and navy became a joke. There were splashes of colour from Jean Muir and Bella Pollen, but it was mostly reserved for evening wear and full-time

mothers. Even sportswear assumed a uniform of black lycra, with zappy fluorescent stripes, nothing too garish, just the connotation of professional standard and ability. Leisurewear was strictly Ivy league and something not too embarrassing if you ran into the boss. Again, American influences excelled, sending the right messages of 'work hard, play hard' priorities. The spectator aspect was the most memorable one, being watched receiving lavish hospitality, watching the best fixtures was the big prize.

In the late 90s where the fixation became retro and lingerie, the 80s are just being resuscitated as a look. The word is that Chanel can't supply enough gilt chain bags, the mini and the jacket are indispensable, and a new obsession with tailoring and Savile Row is infiltrating the market again. Ballgowns have been less in evidence, although, for the real players on the charity ball and country house circuit, they never really went away. When the fickle and fashionable decamped and played bag-woman, those to the Couture house born kept ordering their suits from Valentino, Catherine Walker and Dior, because that for them, was real life. There are even women at the top banks who never gave up the 70s version of 'dress for success' and the pussy-cat bow.

No-one wears a suit to be taken seriously now and the notion of investment in fashion today is a vintage couture gown. The New Victorian mentality came unstuck with the unpaid mortgages and failed Royal marriages. It is quite painful to remember all the issues of the 80s look; the fashion cycle comes round to repeat itself sooner these days, so it is already back for reappraisal by its original exponents. Now that we have dispensed with all the swagged curtains, the hand-made kitchens and the veiled hats, it seems funny to see the other components on their own. It is a bit close for comfort now, but it will be fun to tell your grandchildren in a wry tone, that if you didn't power dress in the 80s, you weren't really there.

left A New York bus carries a series of images during the Calvin Klein jeans campaign of 1995

below Catwalk models including Kate Moss (centre) showing some 'safety pin' dresses by Gianni Versace in February 1994

the trainer as fashion footwear 15

Throughout the 1970s the athletic boom gained momentum and fashion entered the gym – with the traditional leotard and sport shoe being replaced with trendier colourful Spandex activewear and glamorous logoed sport/fashion hybrids. But it was not until 1980 that the gym came into fashion. It was April 1980 and a subway strike in New York led to thousands of workers wearing their training shoes out on the street in order to walk to work. The trend stuck and New Yorkers started to wear the sport shoe with suits and fur coats if any walking was involved. The trainer was out on show and the fashion business had to take notice.

The evolution of sports style had been going on since the early 1970s; the fitness craze led to developments in fabric technology and designers adopted the active spirit and cashed in on the boom. The gym became a place to show off the latest cropped tops, Lycra bodywear and branded sweatshirts but the footwear remained functional and exciting styling was kept to a minimum. Training shoes were basically designed for and worn by sports enthusiasts, and little attention was paid to them outside of the sports arena. The disco look of the late 1970s influenced modern gym apparel by bringing with it an electric colour palette and high shine fabrics such as satin and nylon. This was an influence that would prevail and when the trainer finally did hit the street in 1980 it picked up on the disco theme.

Once the trainer was out on the street the sports shoe manufacturers were forced to co-ordinate the technological developments of the field with stylistic developments that kept them ahead of the pack. Bright colour highlights, hi-tech fabrications and bold logos were a pre-requisite in trying to attain major market share in this new fashion growth area and the big players quickly established themselves as contenders for world domination of the fashion trainer market. Nike, Reebok, Puma and Adidas became the key names and innovators with massive marketing budgets forcing them ahead in the popularity stakes. The fitness boom continued to gain momentum into the new decade with aerobics studios and dance centres developing the atmosphere of the gym into a more fun, sociable venue in which one could spend leisure time. A healthy lifestyle was an new focus and many different types of sport and adventure activity became accessible in the 80s. It was also a time for healthy pursuits in the home and in 1982 Jane Fonda's first workout video was released. It was much copied and a boom started with everyone trying out a little bit of exercise – if not in the gym then at least on the living room floor.

But in the early 1980s an external force evolved that was to contribute significantly to the success or failure of the big brand trainer launches – the phenomenon of Hip-Hop.

Hip-Hop and its associated fashion, art and social message had been an underground force in black American culture since the late 70s. Its pioneers adopted the showy glitz of black disco music but soon the style of the sportsfield with its many black heroes was combined in a look that was completely unique and was entirely Hip-Hop. The showmanship of the music business was evident in the glamour of leather jackets and bold jewellery, but the street conscious subtext of Hip-Hop's vocal message was manifested in the adoption of sportswear as part of the look – with track and field pursuits being a major focus for young black kids whose prospects in life were limited. Hip-Hop as a genre gained momentum into the early 80s and its style was adopted as a mainstream statement of youth fashion everywhere. Its heroes wore their brands with pride, indiscriminately cherrypicking from the latest launches, switching brand allegiance from month to month. They even wore their trainers differently; street styled with laces undone and logoed tongues on show. All of this pushed the sports brands to further develop their styling to incorporate some of street style customizations into new products that featured fatter laces, higher tops and bolder logos. The need for newness was self perpetuating and the more the brands innovated and tried to keep up, the more the Hip-Hop world hyped the war of the brands.

Hip-Hop's stars talked about the latest trainer craze in their raps and publicity shots focused heavily on their footwear fetish. Run DMC's 'Walk This Way' single cover was amongst the most famous of these images; featuring Adidas as the brand of choice. Every time a new release came out the pressure to emulate the image of the performer was renewed. The filtering down of the trend did not take long to occur, and soon kids everywhere were wearing trainers. The football terrace 'casuals' of England in the early 80s had historically fought their fights over fashion as well as team worship. Tottenham Hotspurs 'dressers' sported Burberry macs and smart brogues to the game, while Liverpool's local scallies wore designer button-down shirts and heavy wedge haircuts as a statement of allegiance. But now they were all warring in the trainer stakes. A casual uniform of spectator sportswear was adopted by all and attentions were focused on just making sure you had the latest trainers on. Hip-Hop's music message was of no interest to them but the fashion statement had certainly created a stir.

previous page Grunge icon the late Kurt Cobain of Nirvana sporting 'old skool' low-tech trainers

right Rap superstar Run DMC in his Adidas Super Stars – also known as 'shell toes' – in 1986

Always quick to catch onto a trend or a new youth movement Vivienne Westwood and Malcolm McClaren were probably the first style svengalis to switch the tempo up a gear and to feature trainers at a high fashion level. Westwood's classic Buffalo collection featured designer footwear that mimicked the heavy sole and open laces of streetstyle trainers. McClaren's Hip-Hop inspired single 'Buffalo Girls' featured the same collection in his video and a subsequent singe, 'Double Dutch', featured authentic Hip-Hop beats along with a troupe of dancers wearing heavy trainers and hi-tech tracksuits.

The trainer bug gained momentum through the 1980s; companies such as Nike having to work harder and harder to make fashion statements of new trainers and with marketing getting ever more lifestyle-oriented while still appealing to the real athletes and gymgoers. Styling became more extravagant and futurist and the novelty feature was the designer's route to temporary success. Puma's cell trainers featured clear neon tubular cells around heel and toe in a Bladerunner style sci-fi shoe. Fila's Muscleball trainers took on the appearance of a wheel attached to the foot and Nike's Air Jordan had fashionable python effect panels on the sides. Their later Nike Air Max featured neon tubes in the sole and fitted around the foot like a piece of soft armour and the popular Reebok Airostep looked like cyber-esque fantasy footwear. All of these examples were classics of their time and sales of fashionable trainers had reached epidemic levels by the late 90s. This is when high fashion took notice and decided that it was time for street style to influence the style elite.

above A high-tech model from Puma, one of the key names in trainers past and present

above Converse All Stars, 1990s trainers endorsed by the American basketball star Dennis Rodman

left One of the Vivienne Westwood 'Buffalo Girls' from 1982, the first to feature trainers on the catwalk

left From Karl Lagerfeld, launched during the Chanel collection for Autumn/Winter 91/92

below C. Kitzmantel trainers issued to the Austrian Army and a huge cult hit among aficionados